Moving Forward *with*

RTI

Moving Forward *with*

RTI

Reading & Writing Activities for Every Instructional Setting & Tier

Small-Group Instruction, Independent Application, Partner Work, Whole-Group Engagement, and Small-Group Collaboration

Mary Howard

Foreword by Sharon Taberski

HEINEMANN
Portsmouth, NH

Heinemann
361 Hanover Street
Portsmouth, NH 03801–3912
www.heinemann.com

Offices and agents throughout the world

Library of Congress Cataloging-in-Publication Data
Howard, Mary
    Moving forward with RTI : reading and writing activities for every instructional setting and tier: small-group instruction, independent application, partner work, whole-group engagement, and small-group collaboration / Mary Howard.
        p. cm.
    Includes bibliographical references.
    ISBN-13: 978-0-325-03040-1
    ISBN-10: 0-325-03040-5
    1. Problem children—Education—United States. 2. Behavior disorders in children—United States. 3. Learning disabled children—Education—United States. I. Title.
LC4802.H67 2010
371.9'0446—dc22   2010016306

Editor: Wendy Murray
Production: Lynne Costa
Cover design: Lisa A. Fowler
Text design: Gina Poirier
Typesetter: Gina Poirier
Illustrations: Rita Lascaro
Manufacturing: Steve Bernier

Printed in the United States of America on acid-free paper
14 13 12 11 10   ML   1 2 3 4 5

This book is dedicated to the remarkable children
who initiated almost four decades of
a passionate quest for understanding literacy
and continue to power *new thinking.*

Contents

Foreword

by Sharon Taberski

Perhaps I shouldn't admit to this but I've been known to stalk people I admire. I once found out where Jerome Bruner lived and went to his street, walked past his house—just to look, and pay tribute to the great man within. I know, behavior more befitting a rock star groupie than an upstanding educator, but there you have it.

I stalked Mary Howard once—I guess you'd call it stalking—following her into an elevator years and years ago after her presentation at a state reading conference to ask her for more information on what she'd presented: "Dr. Howard, what exactly does brain research suggest is a wise amount of time to let children read independently? Dr. Howard, I didn't quite get a chance to write down that last quote you shared. Where can I find it?" She was very gracious. And just a few months ago I drove four hours after teaching all day to attend one of Mary's workshops. You get the picture. When I spot talent, I'm like a heat-seeking missile.

And so, as you can imagine, I'm thrilled to finally have easy access to Mary's ideas, first from her best-selling *RTI from All Sides: What Every Teacher Needs to Know* and now from *Moving Forward with RTI: Reading and Writing Activities for Every Instructional Setting and Tier*. If you're a teacher trying to incorporate RTI into your day-to-day classroom practices, but you don't quite know how to manage it, then this book will be a cherished, well-guarded resource you'll want to chain to your desk.

What I like most about Mary's concrete ideas and student response forms is that while they are open-ended, they give the teacher astounding guidance. Sorted by suggested instructional settings in which to use them, they help the teacher *see* the flow of their daily teaching—or create an effective, efficient flow from demonstration to guided practice to independent work. These aren't keep-'em-busy worksheets but thoughtful, smart activities that get children thinking.

Dr. Howard explains the who, what, and why of these activities so busy teachers can more easily use these forms purposefully. Selecting them and adapting them for their students, teachers gain much more than research-based management tools: They gain experience in designing and reteaching lessons so that their students experience learning as an active process—not a passive one.

Mary understands that students need to interact with the ideas, information, and skills and strategies they're trying to learn. As educators, we need to keep in mind that the many students who are working below standards might be stuck in that rut because we haven't sufficiently engaged them. Mary's book is a positive, potent answer to that problem. She provides a wealth of ideas and strategies to help wake up learning and expectations every day. I admire how these activities build each child's personal accountability for learning, but also how they beautifully tune in to kids' developmental needs. They let kids be kids, from the cute illustrations to the fun interactions around texts and ideas that they invite.

Mary Howard, both in her presentation style and her writing, tells it like it is. Don't expect her to sugarcoat an issue. She's upfront and honest. And so when she opens this book by telling readers that the key factor in RTI's success is the "you factor," teachers—all of us—should sit up and take notice. It's what *we* do with a program or activity that can make or break its effectiveness. It's up to us to know our students so we can decide how to best use the lessons and experiences she shares in her book.

Because I've been such a fan of Howard, I know about her background. She is someone who has been in the field working tirelessly with teachers and schools all over the United States and has a deep background in special education—and it all permeates this work. She knows children and teachers so well. The most impressive news of all? Now that she's a book author, if you're interested in learning more about moving forward with Response to Intervention, you won't have to stalk Mary Howard to get the information.

Sharon Taberski is the author of *On Solid Ground: Strategies for Teaching Reading K–3* (2000) and *Comprehension from the Ground Up: Simplified, Sensible Instruction for the K–3 Reading Workshop* (2010)

Acknowledgments

A book is a remarkable venture that requires many people who contribute in a variety of ways. I want to thank my sister, brothers, nieces, and nephews for their unwavering support as I traveled from coast to coast and wrote long hours during my limited time at home. I am grateful for the guidance of my incredible editor, Wendy Murray, and the talent and support of everyone at Heinemann. The beautiful cover design and every page in between could not happen without their hard work behind the scenes.

I also want to thank the dedicated teachers with whom I work. They constantly stimulate my thinking about the meaning of literacy in our lives, and how we might go about teaching it. These teachers have been instrumental in developing the practices and activities in this book. They have done them, tweaked them, and turned them into their own iterations, so that I am confident that what I share with you will work in many grades, settings, and instructional contexts. Special thanks goes to the administrators, school leaders, and teachers who graciously allowed me to "borrow" students and contributed to the thoughtful dialogue that helped me fine-tune each activity to ensure maximum benefit.

Kasson Mantorville Elementary in Kasson, Minnesota (Principal, Marsha Groth):

Kelly Braun, Camille Lechnir, Michelle Hamm, Tim Mulrine, Collen Lau, Hedi Diercks, Jody Beckstrom, Alecia Meline, Matt Rasaaen, Micaela Herold, Linda Walbruch, Brian Sandstrom, Jenny Anderson, Dani Gile, Pat Hansen, Diane Lindgren, Ryan Haraldson, Cindy Raaen, Laura Peck, Jody Vossen, Lisa Bronk, Michelle Yotter, Matt Erredge, Stacy Sievers, Nancy Voth, Sharie Furst, Paula Dahms, John Vossen, Jana Southwick, Mary Johnson, Jenny Obst, Curt Naylor, Joel Olsen

Lincoln Elementary in Lawton, Oklahoma (Principal, Robbie Gillis):

Kim Everett, Rebecca Ward, Rebecca Clark, Beth Lane, Jeannie Wilson, Bernadette Richardson, Ruth Ritter, Brandi Knutson, Tara Grandy, Carolyn Poe, Lori Newell

Howell Elementary in Lawton, Oklahoma (Principal, Sharon Havron):

Linda Hayes, Jenny Reinhart, Sarah Bruehl, Tonja Godlewkski, Debra Love, Shelley Cargill, Andrea Neace, Kristy Campbell, Tammy Mooney, Brooke Hyde, Cindy Griffy

Swinney Elementary in Lawton, Oklahoma (Principal, Kathleen Dering):

Karen Blanton, Carol Gardner, Jamie Dwyer, Patsy Stoll, Vera Wahkinney, Norman Lavigne, Judy Lynn, Kathy Traughber

Pat Henry Elementary in Lawton, Oklahoma (Principal, Bill Ingram):

Misty Cefalu, Susan Gannon, Zeida Herrera, Stacey McKinney, Sherry Jaurrieta, Elizabeth Smith, Rebel Burkhalter, Ann Johnson, Sandi Weatherly, Kathey Brashear, Kim Bleau, Oscar Castro, Ann Love, Staci Walker, Debbie Payne, Nancy Breaden, Neyra Montero, Vicki Blanchard, Kerri Franz, Deborah Harrel, Deborah Wrensford

Bishop Elementary in Lawton, Oklahoma (Superintendent/Principal, Howard Hampton; Assistant Principal, Christie Tugmon):

Lori Baggett, Belinda Macks, Mary Anne Sanders, Sheila Corbett, Laura Mansel, Darla Nunley, Kayla Durgin, Michelle Churchwell, Kristy Duty, Denise Burk, Elizabeth Martin, Jennifer Schoolfield, Shelly Penrod, Josie Marcum

The Key to RTI

Getting Smarter About the Instructional Interplay Between Whole-Group, Small-Group, and Independent Learning

There's no such thing as the perfect lesson, the perfect day in school, or the perfect teacher. For teachers and students alike, the goal is not perfection but persistence in the pursuit of understanding things.

(Tomlinson and McTighe 2006, 56)

"Mary, of all of the things you've shared today, what is most important?" the principal at Kasson-Mantorville Elementary School in Kasson, Minnesota, asks me. All the teachers in the room turn to look at me. I have spent the day here to help them design the most effective Response to Intervention (RTI) framework. We've discussed many critical factors such as scheduling, group size, and instructional goals linked to assessment—but without missing a beat I declare, "The *you* factor!" as I sweep my arm to acknowledge the teachers. "If we ever hope to accomplish excellence, these dedicated teachers at this table matter most."

"Honestly," I continue. "*You* are the key piece. The fact that you view the quest to understand more about teaching and learning as rewarding and something you do day after day—well, that's what is going to help your students achieve in literacy."

Whenever I work with teachers, the *you* factor is what I want them to take most seriously. That is, their dedication, smarts, creativity, knowledge of each student—all of it combines to create a literacy environment in which students thrive. Sure, I advise on group size, classroom environment, and differentiation, but none of these is comparable to the role of each teacher. We can have two children in a group, but it won't guarantee effective instruction. We can design a breathtaking classroom, but it won't guarantee best practice. Literacy excellence is never about whether we elect to use a particular program or approach. Without exception, the key is how richly teachers implement these programs and approaches—a feat that only happens when teachers feel empowered to maintain a central role.

In my first book, *RTI from All Sides*, I described the merits and potential missteps of Response To Intervention. At the heart of that book was my conviction that the expertise and engagement of regular classroom teachers would make or break the success of RTI in catching readers at risk. As I heard from teachers who read my book, I pondered what educators learning about RTI and differentiation needed next to support them. What was one of their biggest challenges in teaching reading and writing? It didn't take long to reach a conclusion—they needed to be able to keep twenty or thirty children engaged in learning for just about every minute of the day. One second-grade teacher told me she kept students in rows with whole-group learning all day because she was terrified to manage small-groups. Others feared children would learn little if left to work independently. It seemed apparent that fear was feeding their struggle to differentiate.

This book offers a wide range of flexible, high-quality literacy activities that can be used in any grade level or instructional context or setting—including whole-group, guided practice, small-group, partner work, and independent learning. I designed the activities with the *you* factor in mind. That is, they help *you* be the expert. I do not spoon-feed scripts or mandate a lockstep approach. Prescribed lessons are not needed "because our knowledgeable observations have given us a detailed sense of how and what to teach" (Owocki 2010, 293). *You* decide when to use them and how to adapt them based on *your* knowledge of students. Each strategy is designed to support the differentiation that underlies an effective RTI framework with flexible activities that will:

DEEPEN STUDENTS' UNDERSTANDING. A student form accompanies each activity so that the children's written responses help them review and deepen what they've learned. These responses give you insight into how to provide students with feedback and ongoing support.

SUPPORT A GRADUAL RELEASE OF RESPONSIBILITY MODEL. Each form highlights the *to*, *with*, and *by* framework. That is, teachers demonstrate and think aloud as they complete a form in front of students, conduct shared activities with students, initiate guided activities with decreasing support, and organize peer-supported and independent activities. Throughout this book, you will begin to visualize a recursive movement of modeled, shared, and guided practice or independent learning for just the right level of support needed at just the right moment.

PROVIDE AN OPPORTUNITY FOR HIGH-LEVEL DISCUSSION. The forms make reading and writing a springboard for using discussion to exchange ideas in meaningful ways. Oral language is an often overlooked facet of comprehension (Taberski 2009). When students articulate their developing understandings about texts, concepts, or words, it helps them solidify this knowledge as they learn from their peers. Discussion allows you to use conversations to gauge children's levels of understanding as you become more instructionally responsive.

ENCOURAGE CROSS-CURRICULAR CONNECTIONS. The open-ended forms are designed to work with any text across all content areas. As students use the same form across two or more subjects they will begin to see the connections between various learning activities of their school day. This instructional interplay reinforces learning and promotes transfer.

SUPPORT THE TIERED INSTRUCTION OF RTI. These activities are ideal for tier 1 classroom instruction, but they are easily adjusted for tier 2 and tier 3, when more intensity and teacher support are needed. Further, they support the goals of helping students become self-regulating, independent learners—fostering collaboration and motivation, outcomes to create a learning environment that lifts up weaker readers like a rising tide.

GIVE STUDENTS BRIEF, CONNECTED LEARNING SESSIONS OVER TIME. Students can complete a form during one instructional activity if time is available, but you can also break learning into smaller, meaningful tasks that students complete across one week. When we stretch a learning experience over several days, students benefit from revisiting their work before moving on to the next learning challenge as we reinforce previous efforts and promote new learning and connect known to new.

PROMOTE AUTHENTIC LITERACY EXPERIENCES. The forms allow students to practice skills in the context of your curriculum's meaningful reading and writing, rather than in isolation. For example, in most cases the teacher introduces an activity using a read-aloud to lay the foundation (with teacher modeling or think-aloud). The teacher then selects varied texts in alternative settings, and adjusts support according to the needs of students.

PROVIDE A RICH SOURCE OF ASSESSMENT. Assessment and instruction are inseparable. Informal assessments are provided so that teachers can take the pulse of their own teaching to reflect on how much students are learning. These assessments combine with other informal observations of children to help teachers plan their subsequent lessons, as each learning experience offers a new opportunity to assess.

A Visual Tour of the Instructional Settings

The focus of this book is quite simple. Begin with your curriculum goals and use the forms as the conduit to promote those goals with activities that integrate reading and writing through engaging discussion and collaboration, as shown at right.

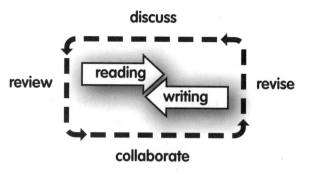

An effective RTI design acknowledges the broad-based nature of the tier 1 classroom as teachers differentiate in a wide range of flexible settings and contexts to meet students' needs. This wider instructional lens includes whole-group instruction while making room for teacher-supported, peer-supported, and independent learning experiences. Remember, *you know what works best for your students.* And your ability to reflect on and use this knowledge is at the heart of RTI. The activities in this book do not dictate content, but are instead vehicles to help you structure your delivery of content. *You* make the activities work by choosing the just-right texts, the most engaging words, or a topic of study that is best suited for your curriculum goals and your students' needs.

The icons shown on the next page are used throughout this book to help you consider these varied settings as you select each activity. The settings you select are based on your professional judgment given your curriculum goals and students' current learning needs.

WHOLE-GROUP ENGAGEMENT allows you to introduce, model, or initiate your learning activities. These experiences must allow at least 80 percent of your students to perform at proficiency (Dorn and Schubert 2008). Whole-class engagement will build a solid foundation for other settings that follow. Some students will need far more support at this stage than others.

SMALL-GROUP COLLABORATION makes room for peer-supported learning with shared teacher support. Students work together to put new learning in action as you rotate to offer support as needed. This phase of shared learning starts students on the path to increasing independence.

SMALL-GROUP INSTRUCTION allows more intensive teacher support, such as guided reading. Use this time to modify the activity by aligning learning to your readers. These flexible groups offer targeted instruction in meaningful contexts using carefully selected texts.

PARTNER WORK is a good transition from the more intensive support that we offer before students work independently (Fisher and Frey 2008). This provides time to complete activities with peers at increasing levels of independence and to initiate dialogue that promotes and reinforces thinking.

INDEPENDENT APPLICATION gives students time to apply learning on their own. This reinforcement and extension allows students to achieve high levels of success without teacher support and is essential to learning. Students need many of these successful experiences on a daily basis.

Some Tips for Ensuring the Activities Stay Dynamic

Over time, you'll see how these activities help you understand and manage instructional differentiation. As time passes, adapt the activities based on your growing knowledge of your students.

These forms must also be accompanied with cautionary advice. I've watched excellent ideas turn into passive activities students do with little thought, and I don't want these forms to suffer the same fate. Here are some tips to maximize the social nature of learning through engaging tasks carefully matched to student needs.

✴ Provide students with clear guidelines. They need to feel confident with both the activity and the peer and self-assessment procedures.

✴ Always begin by modeling to ensure that students understand the thinking process first. There will be times when students don't need teacher modeling at all, and times when you will offer more intensive support over days or even weeks before students are ready to take over independently.

* Your continued involvement is essential, whether to model or support student efforts. Emphasize collaboration or side-by-side learning as you rotate among students as they work. Dialogue and interaction revolving around these forms will keep them from becoming static worksheets students plod through on their own. That is not the spirit or intent of the forms.

* The forms require your meaningful, ongoing feedback. This has nothing to do with happy faces, stickers, or red marks but how you interact with students throughout learning. Look for the teachable moment at every stage of learning, when you craft what you say to bring the student to a higher level of understanding with supportive accountability.

* Learn about your students by encouraging them to verbalize thinking and use this to probe ("What do you mean?" "Tell me more," "Give me an example"). Your thoughtful questioning will provide important information that will support instructional decision making through learning.

* These activities require texts at appropriate levels of difficulty. Emphasize brief texts that are interesting, appealing, and well written, rather than selections that are too long or challenging. Your choices can inhibit or enrich learning. Always opt for the latter.

* Meet the needs of students who struggle by gathering them to complete the forms in smaller, more intensive instructional settings. This repeated practice and teacher support will level the playing field by providing the just-right instruction they need and deserve and continued success when you begin to relinquish support. This varies from student to student.

Imagine for a moment that you are holding a lightbulb in your hands. The lightbulb is a remarkable design, but it has little use without a power source. When it is connected to a power source, the lightbulb is instantly illuminated. In the same way, the forms and activity ideas I've created are simply the lightbulb in your hand—but they are useless without a power source. Once again, the *you* factor comes into play as *you* power the ideas by carefully choosing just the right text, context, setting, and dialogue most likely to lead to learning. As you share these activities with your students, never lose sight of the fact that *you* power learning events—and the light shines ever more radiantly the more you engage in the instructional process. Quite an amazing design concept, isn't it?

Developing Independent Literacy

Daily Rituals

Putting the RTI model into practice means that you allow students to work independently at various times throughout the day. In order to ensure that this time is instructionally rich, you need consistent structures that students can follow without the support of the teacher. Many teachers have asked me, "While I am busy teaching individual students and small groups, what are the other students doing?" In this chapter, you will find daily routines that engage students in activities for building independent literacy.

These routines offer rituals that are designed to reinforce rather than teach, and should emphasize activities that increase the volume of reading and writing. They don't replace your existing management procedures, such as literacy centers, but extend and support those procedures by promoting students' sustained independent literacy engagement. These rituals also serve a second and essential goal of RTI—to allow you to work uninterrupted in more intensive settings so that you can provide the targeted instruction that will help other students move to the next level. Begin teaching daily rituals early in the year so that you can initiate small-group experiences as soon as possible.

Activities at a Glance

Here is a quick reference to the activities you'll find in this section.

Daily Choice Folder

A collection of five valuable literacy activities from which students may choose daily.

> **Setting:** Partner and independent
>
> **Instructional Focus:** *reading, writing about reading,* and *writing to support learning*
>
> **Forms:** My Daily Choice Folder Activities, My Daily Choice Folder Record

Weekly Independent Reading Options

A collection of daily independent reading activities identified by visuals.

> **Setting:** Partner and independent
>
> **Instructional Focus:** *reading, writing about reading*
>
> **Forms:** Weekly Independent Reading Options, Weekly Independent Reading Cards

Golden Book Basket Response

Students recommend a favorite text in writing to encourage new readers.

> **Setting:** Whole-group, partner, and independent
>
> **Instructional Focus:** *reading, writing about reading*
>
> **Forms::** Golden Book Basket Response

Daily Choice Folder

What It Is

A Daily Choice Folder provides students with immediate access to a variety of literacy activities. The term *choice* is essential: students can look at the options listed on their folders and choose any authentic, high-success activity they want to complete. Selections are based on a discussion between the teacher and students about meaningful reading and writing activities worthy of the folder. The "Daily Choice Record" in their folder then provides a space for students to record their selected activities daily and to self-assess their weekly progress.

Instructional Focus

reading, writing about reading, writing to support learning

When to Use It

The folder can be used in a variety of ways: to open the day, when other independent literacy tasks are completed, to close the day, or during any open blocks of time.

What to Do

1. Discuss with your students engaging ways they can practice their reading and writing. Offer some ideas and get their buy in! Students often chime in with free choice reading, writing in their journal, enjoying a poetry folder, or discussing a favorite book with classmates. Work together to select five activities that you can focus on for the entire year. The open-ended nature of activities will offer something for everyone. Read, Listen, and Think (described on page 77) or buddy reading are two examples of activities that are open-ended enough for kids to do all year. You can augment the activities as time goes on. For example, as you use the Daily Choice Folder, students may suggest a "Bright Idea" to add to the right side of the form. As long as the activity meets the same criteria you've set (meaningful reading and writing), it's fine for the student to add an idea. Discussion should always revolve around these additions.

2. Prepare pocket folders for each child by attaching a blank "My Daily Choice Folder Activities" form to the front of the folder and place the "My Daily Choice Folder Record" inside the folder. Students use the forms as a reference for activity options and also to self-assess their progress weekly.

3. Demonstrate how to complete each activity you've chosen, and invite students to contribute ideas so that you can assess that they understand what to do and can do them independently, with high engagement. Be sure to help them select just right texts and writing topics that are interesting.

continues

Teaching Tips

* The folder can serve as a springboard for discussions that revolve around varied reading and writing. For example, students' self-assessment can help you recognize their strengths and weaknesses as well as what topics they are interested in.

* Don't worry if a student wishes to complete the same activity each day for weeks. Time students spend reading or writing is always time well spent, particularly when motivation is high.

* Periodically, revisit the Daily Choice Folder as a class. Invite students' thoughts on how their work is helping them become stronger readers and writers. What's going well? What's more challenging? What kinds of things do they like most? Are they selecting texts and topics they find interesting?

* You may create problem-solving charts *with* students to address challenges. For example, if students are having a hard time selecting a journal focus or text, brainstorm ideas. Avoid simply listing starter sentences or titles, opting to help students explore personal interests. These charts are based on your observations and discussions with students and should support independence throughout the school day.

Daily Choice Folder *(continued)*

4. When students use the Daily Choice Folder, each child will circle the activity rituals completed each day at the top of the "Daily Choice Folder Record." At the end of the week, students self-assess their efforts on their own, with a partner, or with the teacher. This is a good opportunity to draw attention to text selection, interest, and engagement.

5. During the year, you may add to or update the Bright Ideas on the right side of the folder. This is a good way to discuss students' role. For example, students may create a word game using personal word goals for practice and reinforcement or create class or peer books for reading. It is important to increase their accountability and involvement.

6. Periodically, meet with students as a class to debrief activities to emphasize student accountability. You may work together to establish goals so that students are involved in evaluating their own progress as independent learners. These discussions will also provide the teacher with valuable assessment information.

My Daily Choice Folder Activities

Name _____

1

2

3

4

5

Bright Idea

My Daily Choice Folder Record

Name _____ **Week of** _____

Monday	Tuesday	Wednesday	Thursday	Friday
1	1	1	1	1
2	2	2	2	2
3	3	3	3	3
4	4	4	4	4
5	5	5	5	5
Bonus	**Bonus**	**Bonus**	**Bonus**	**Bonus**

These activities helped me to learn how to _____

_____

_____

I used my time well this week by _____

_____

_____

The activity I liked doing most this week was _____

_____

because _____

Weekly Independent Reading Options

What It Is

If you wish to focus on a wider range of daily reading rituals, use the Weekly Independent Reading Options for a visual overview of a wider range of daily independent reading activities. Students can track and organize these independent activities by color-coding completed tasks. They then self-evaluate their progress at the end of each week. This concrete reference provides an excellent resource for teacher and peer conferencing.

Instructional Focus

reading, writing about reading

When to Use It

These options may be preferable for the early grades. Visuals offer a quick reference for activity options making it easier for beginning readers to identify the daily selections and color coding increases accountability.

What to Do

1. Introduce the form and select one or two activities to model and discuss. As you introduce each activity, make a copy of the matching option card to display. This makes it easy to highlight specific selections. Brainstorm key features of the activity, such as activity options (read alone or with a partner), selection of resources (can you read the book without help?), and guidelines (noise level and appropriate rules). These are important details that will help to ensure that students are meaningfully engaged without the support of the teacher.

2. When you first introduce each activity, all students should complete that activity at the same time. As students begin working, rotate through the room to observe. Use your observations to debrief or discuss specific adjustments to ensure quality implementation of that activity. Show students how to color-code completed activities.

3. Create a wall display to showcase reading activities using the Weekly Independent Reading Cards. You can individualize selections by using name cards that can be moved. You may also add a photograph of students engaged in each activity to personalize reading options and provide a visual reminder.

4. At the end of the week, each student will complete the self-evaluation at the bottom of the form. It is important to provide time for students to discuss their evaluations in whole-group, partner, or teacher conferences. If quality time is not spent working independently as you work in small groups, it is simply wasted time—so continuously revisit and discuss these experiences.

continues

Teaching Tips

* The details of the activities can be recorded with a visual on 8½-by-11-inch cards and placed in a three-ring binder for reference. This may include photographs of students engaged in the activity with student samples as appropriate. These details are important to ensure the quality of the activities. No detail is too trivial to address.

* Provide time for students to discuss their personal reading goals and successes with the teacher or each other. These discussions are important since students are constantly building greater independence as they are actively engaged in meaningful and worthwhile activity selections.

* Do not lose sight of the role of student choice. Be sure to identify those options that must be scheduled such as traveling reader vs. those that are open to student selection. Motivation increases as students maintain more control.

Description of Weekly Reading Options

(*) Starred items are scheduled weekly

Independent Reading: Students read any text from the reading center. The teacher needs to make sure that ample texts are available at each student's independent reading level.

Book Bag Reading: Students select a book from their individual collection, usually kept in a bag for transport between school and home. These include selections previously read in teacher-supported guided reading and identified as meriting repeated reading.

Poetry Basket: Students self-select favorite classroom poetry that has been introduced by the teacher for repeated reading.

Fluency Folder: A folder is filled with brief collections of familiar texts, songs, reader's theater scripts, or other classroom favorites for fluency practice.

* Guest Reader: Two or more guest readers (parent volunteers or students from a higher grade) come to the classroom daily so each child can read with a partner weekly.

* Traveling Reader: Students sign up to practice a brief text to read in another classroom (generally at a lower grade level). Students in the receiving class can then compliment the reader.

Buddy Reading: Students take turns reading a familiar selection to a partner sitting face-to-face so the focus is on listening over following along.

* Read to the Teacher: Students read a self-selected text to the teacher weekly for feedback and informal assessment information.

* Recording Center: Students record a selection (see "Read, Listen, and Think" on page 77).

* Listening Center: Students will listen to a story weekly from the listening library.

Golden Book Response: Students complete a book recommendation to share with the class, other classrooms, or the teacher.

Golden Book Reading: Students read books that are recommended by the class, other classrooms, or the teacher. Selection options are collected in a labeled container such as a basket.

Weekly Independent Reading Options

Name _____ Week of _____

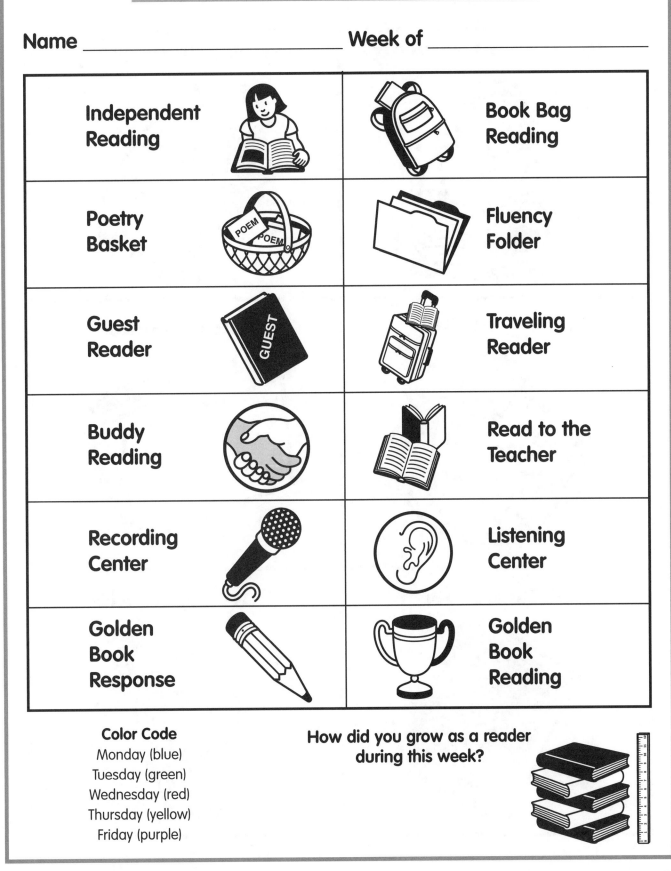

Independent Reading		**Book Bag Reading**	
Poetry Basket		**Fluency Folder**	
Guest Reader		**Traveling Reader**	
Buddy Reading		**Read to the Teacher**	
Recording Center		**Listening Center**	
Golden Book Response		**Golden Book Reading**	

Color Code
Monday (blue)
Tuesday (green)
Wednesday (red)
Thursday (yellow)
Friday (purple)

How did you grow as a reader during this week?

Weekly Independent Reading Cards

Independent Reading	Book Bag Reading
Poetry Basket	Fluency Folder
Guest Reader	Traveling Reader

Weekly Independent Reading Cards

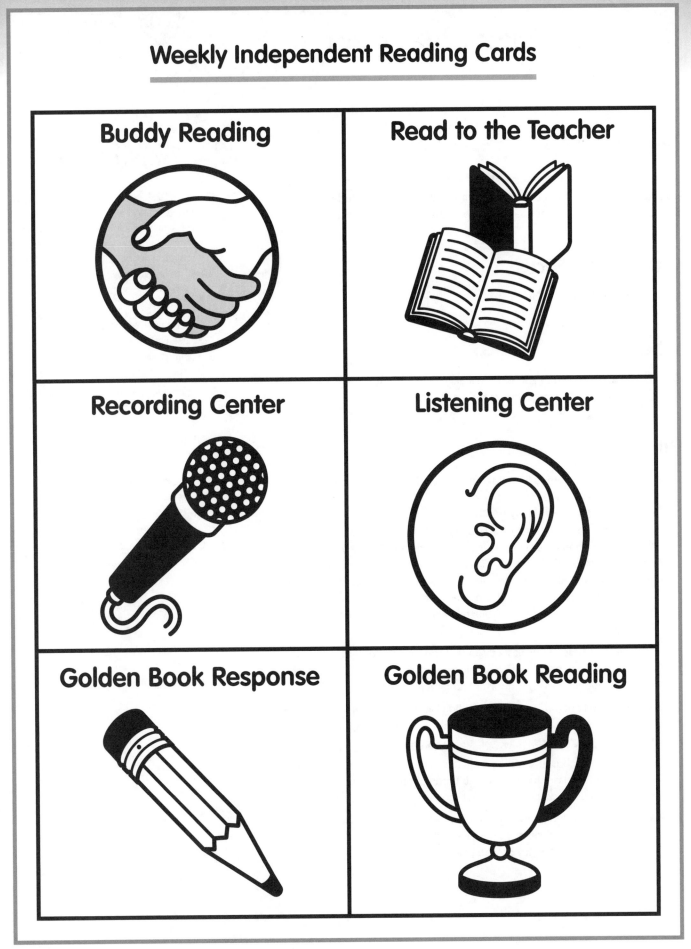

Buddy Reading

Read to the Teacher

Recording Center

Listening Center

Golden Book Response

Golden Book Reading

Golden Book Basket Response

What It Is

A Golden Book Basket Response allows students to recommend a personal favorite selection they deem worthy of this high distinction. Students use the form to record and share their selections with the classroom or peers.

Instructional Focus

reading, writing about reading

When to Use It

This activity may be used as part of the Weekly Independent Reading Options as well as to advertise and discuss books throughout the day.

What to Do

1. Spray-paint a basket metallic gold and attach a sign reading *Our Golden Book Basket*. Explain to students that this basket will be used to hold those books that students think are simply the "best of the best." Generate some criteria with students that might make a book earn its golden status. Because it is hilarious? Has a great protagonist? Beautiful language? Is highly informative? Has beautiful images? Great topic? There are no wrong answers, for these are personal favorites. Also generate a list of possible genres that might make it into the basket, from poetry to photo-filled animal books. The only sure criterion is that the child has read the selection and believes that her peers would enjoy it as well.

2. Hand out the Golden Book Basket Winner form to each student. Tell them to think about a book they want to nominate for this distinction. This teacher-supported modeling will be important for later independence.

3. The next day, fill out forms as a class, guiding kids to help them fill out the various sections. Verbalize your thinking or probe for details as appropriate.

4. Ask for volunteers to share the Golden Book Basket recommendations orally on a daily basis. This is an excellent way to use meaningful reading and writing to build enthusiasm for reading and broaden selections for new readers. Encourage peers to ask questions about the recommendations.

5. Place the Golden Book Basket recommendations in the book and display them in the basket. Students may self-select their own or other books for reading either independently or with peers.

Teaching Tips

* Form Golden Book Basket discussion groups during which students can do a book talk on their pick and respond to questions. You may also form groups to initiate engaging discussions among students who have read a common text for discussion and extension.

* Share text selections beyond the classroom by creating a Traveling Golden Book Basket. These student recommendations can travel to other classrooms to inspire other readers.

* Encourage parents, teachers, and staff to create traveling Golden Book Baskets. The librarian may recommend books that are new to the library or wonderful treasures students do not know about. The principal or staff members may create a basket of books they loved as children. Parents may recommend books they read to their children. This is a wonderful way to demonstrate reading for pleasure while modeling that reading is a worthy personal pursuit.

Golden Book Basket Response

Fold the completed book form in half and insert in the selected book

Golden Book Basket Winner

WINNER

Nominated by:

_____

Title

_____

Author

_____

I love this book because

_____

_____

_____

You should read it because

_____

_____

_____

My Summary Hook

My Picture Peek

Encouraging Personal Accountability

Learning Reflections

How many times do parents ask their children "What did you learn today?" only to hear the words "Nothing!" or "I don't remember." While this classic response is more material for an Erma Bombeck piece on parenting than cause for alarm, it does give us reason to wonder: Is what we teach during the day memorable enough? Meaningful enough? Would children be more inclined to cite personal learning accomplishments if we gave them regular opportunities to reflect on what they've learned with others? These are certainly questions worth asking.

The activities in this section invite students to reflect on their learning each day through writing and discussion. Students respond to what they learn in writing and then use these reflections as the basis for discussion. The more students are able to articulate their own learning processes, the more we can assess and personalize that learning, and thus make it more relevant and memorable to children. These reflection opportunities can occur at the end of each day, at the conclusion of important topics of learning, or can be embedded in any stage of a learning activity.

Activities at a Glance

Here is a quick reference to the activities you'll find in this section.

Learning Reflection Journal

A journal in which students record and reflect on learning objectives throughout the year.

> **Setting:** Whole-group, small-group collaboration, small-group instruction, partner, and independent
>
> **Instructional Focus:** *writing to support learning, discussion*
>
> **Forms:** My Personal Learning Journal, My Learning Journal Objectives

Student Anchor Chart

Students record classroom learning objectives with the teacher and add new ideas revolving around these concepts in small-group settings using appropriate texts.

> **Setting:** Whole-group, small-group collaboration, and partner
>
> **Instructional Focus:** *writing to support learning, discussion*
>
> **Forms:** Student Anchor Chart, Research Anchor Chart

Personal Daily Reflection Record

Students reflect on the important learning from each day and identify the key concepts they learned that week to share with others.

> **Setting:** Whole-group, partner, and independent
>
> **Instructional Focus:** *writing to support learning, discussion*
>
> **Forms:** Personal Daily Reflection Record

Personal Pondering Pad

Students reflect on what they know, are learning, or wonder about a topic (in written or picture form) before it is discussed in class.

> **Setting:** Whole-group, small-group collaboration, and partner
>
> **Instructional Focus:** *writing to support learning, discussion*
>
> **Forms:** Personal Pondering Pad

Learning Reflection Journal

What It Is

The Learning Reflection Journal is a record of the year's key learning objectives. Objectives may be connected to curriculum goals or identified as areas of need. The journal format serves as a concrete tool to record key points from instructional minilessons to provide a long-term resource for review and extension. The journal also offers a reference to inform and support more intensive small-group activities or for student or parent conferencing.

Instructional Focus

writing to support learning, discussion

When to Use It

The Learning Reflection Journal needs to be used consistently throughout the year to reinforce and extend learning after a concept is introduced. This offers an important learning ritual throughout the year and emphasizes the value of recording and revisiting key ideas.

What to Do

1. Use the Table of Contents page to identify the year's key objectives for one subject. You can create learning journals of different colors to reflect different subjects. Place two Table of Contents pages at the front of each journal with about thirty white unlined pages.

2. Introduce the journal by drawing two side-by-side boxes to reflect an open page (students record this at the front of the journal as a reminder). Label the right side "Listening Notes" and the left side "Brain Notes." "Listening notes" are a place to record key points of direct teacher instruction with an objective number in the top right corner. The objective number quickly identifies an important learning goal listed on the Table of Contents page. "Brain notes" are where students will apply that learning throughout the school year. This allows the teacher to revisit learning goals in a variety of contexts to promote transfer and reinforce learning.

3. The activity begins on the right side of the journal with teacher instruction to introduce an objective. Record the objective number to match the table of contents listing in the top right corner and underlined concept title in the center. If possible use teacher read-aloud to introduce concepts with a text example. Students should listen as you record brief learning points and then copy these key concepts on the right side of their journal. This will be used as

continues

Teaching Tips

* Use the journal to review key concepts regularly in a wide variety of settings. Encourage your students to restate information in the journal for added benefit. This will reinforce learning and make students more accountable by allowing them to personalize what they have learned. This will be easy to do when concepts are recorded in key words rather than sentences.

* Form small groups to discuss key concepts and add new points to take learning to deeper levels. This activity may revolve around common or varied texts as students apply this learning in their reading. Each group can then share what they have added in a whole-group setting to extend and enrich the learning points.

* Encourage students to add quick sketches, visuals, or color-coding to enhance their understanding. Provide time to discuss these important reflections of learning.

a long-term learning reference so it should be brief bulleted points, examples, or definitions students can quickly revisit.

4. After teaching, students will apply learning on the left side with examples. Students may use the Pondering Pad (see description on page 32) before writing ideas in the journal to ensure accuracy since it is a long-term reference. Rotate as students work to support their thinking, or encourage collaboration and discussion. Students add new examples on the left side as they are introduced in new activities. Additional examples are continuously added throughout the year using a variety of resources.

5. Revisit the journal when you find an example that is fitting. For example, during a read-aloud, you might say, "Listen as I read this again. See if you can find a simile to add to our Learning Journal." Or, you could combine independent reading and peer collaboration by saying, "After you read today, find an example of a word with the prefix *un-* to add to your journal. Share this with a partner."

6. Use the journal to review concepts for additional reinforcement or when students need to apply the concept in assessment. A five-minute review activity can significantly enhance a child's absorption of knowledge and understanding.

7. As appropriate, generate lists of words and concepts that can then be organized on a chart (*tion* vs. *sion* words; similes vs. metaphors). Students' role in gathering these lists using authentic personal examples will be far superior to simply supplying a list of words from a publisher.

My Personal Learning Journal

JOURNAL

Name _____   **Teacher/Grade** _____

Subject _____

My Learning Journal Objectives

Table of Contents

Date	Learning Topic	Lesson No.

Student Anchor Chart

What It Is

The Student Anchor Chart is a small-group adaptation of Debbie Miller's classroom anchor charts (Miller 2002) that provide a classroom reference for learning. A Student Anchor Chart allows you to connect classroom instruction to small-group learning activities so that students can apply learning in appropriate texts with support.

Instructional Focus

writing to support learning, discussion

When to Use It

Use this tool to support teacher instruction and as a reference to add new learning in small-group settings or to review learning with peers.

What to Do

1. Select a teaching point that supports your curriculum and student learning goals. This is a concept that all students will need, so provide the initial teaching in the form of a whole-group minilesson. It is preferable to use a meaningful text to support the concept. This may be a brief read-aloud or shared reading activity such as a poem. If you are using a shared reading activity, be sure that it will be a high-success text for all students. The text is simply the conduit for promoting the learning ideas so it must be accessible to every learner.

2. Record the important learning points on the board as students add these ideas to the form. In first grade, you may record simple points on the form in advance and ask students to add a picture. This may include a definition of a concept or key ideas. Always bring this learning back to the text so that you maintain a meaningful context and engage students in discussing these ideas. This may result in rereading key text illustrating ideas.

3. As you meet with students in small-group settings, use the anchor chart to revisit the important ideas. Use a carefully selected text to highlight these same concepts. Students will add new points to the bottom section of the anchor chart. These are examples that support the learning concept—such as words with a particular pattern, literary examples, or specific text samples.

4. After your small-group activities, provide time for students to share their examples with peers. These all revolve around a common instructional activity so the varied examples will provide a wide range of learning opportunities that will reinforce and extend learning as students share different ways of looking at the same concepts using various resources.

Teaching Tips

* At the completion of small-group activities, revisit the concepts as a class. Each group may be asked to restate this learning in its own words and share examples using its text by reading brief portions aloud.

* Use the Research Anchor Chart to focus on a common topic. Introduce the topic with a whole-group read-aloud. Discuss the topic and generate key questions to record at the top of the form. These are general questions that will be relevant to all students. You may also introduce several key words and record these on the bottom left of the form. Every small group will then read a text at an appropriate level on that same topic and respond to the questions or add new words. The "BIG Picture" on the bottom right is a place to record a summary of ideas or create an illustration.

* Create a display revolving around the learning concept. This may include brief summaries of important ideas, definitions, or students' illustrations. The display should reflect in a new way what students have learned and should be used as an ongoing research reference as new ideas are added.

Student Anchor Chart

Lesson Focus _____

Teacher

Personal

Research Anchor Chart

Name _____ **Topic** _____

Q u e s t i o n s

Key Vocabulary

_____

_____

_____

_____

_____

The BIG Picture

Personal Daily Reflection Record

What It Is

The Personal Daily Reflection Record offers a simple way for students to reflect on their learning at the end of each day or following a topic of learning. Students will record that day's learning success ("What made you smarter today?") on the form with a description and illustration if desired. After the form is completed, students can share their success with a peer who adds their initials or name in the box on the right side. At the end of the week, students identify the week's most important success.

Instructional Focus

writing to support learning, discussion

When to Use It

Use this tool at the conclusion of the day or after a topic of learning to end on a positive note that focuses on students' successes.

What to Do

1. At the end of the day, think out loud to demonstrate how you identify your personal learning successes and select one to record on the form. Highlight every aspect of your thinking, including how to write it in a brief statement or add a simple visual. After you complete the form, model how to share your learning with a student as you stand face-to-face. Generally, teacher modeling will continue for one week to ensure students understand the process.

2. Move to a shared format when students are ready. Begin by brainstorming important learning ideas, recording each one as it is suggested. This helps stimulate thinking and supports students who struggle putting their ideas in writing by verbalizing them first.

3. Review the list and emphasize that students will choose learning points specific to their personal role as a learner. Encourage students to record learning in both print and illustrations. Rotate around the room as students complete the form to support their efforts, ask questions, and encourage elaboration or examples.

4. Peer sharing and collaboration is an important part of the activity. Sharing personal learning ideas allows students to celebrate their learning while acknowledging that we all know different things and vary in what we feel is important.

5. Rotate around the room as students share to gain valuable information about what is relevant for them. Since this is a brief activity, students may share with several peers. Encourage partners to ask questions and express appreciation before signing the form. Use this time to take anecdotal records.

6. At the end of the week, students will select the most important learning of the week. Provide time for students to share this learning briefly with a partner as a culmination activity. Encourage partners to discuss the ideas or ask questions.

Teaching Tips

✱   Reverse the order of completing the form as appropriate; some students will find it helpful to share with a partner before they put their ideas in writing or add the illustration first. Allow students to modify the activity in any way needed to support their own thinking.

✱   Use the completed form in student conferencing to probe for more details about learning. Acknowledge what the child feels is important, always maintaining the student's focus with questions that reflect genuine interest while celebrating the child's ideas about relevant learning.

✱   Use an index card in place of the form at the end of the week or specific unit of study as a "Ticket Out the Door" activity. On one side of the index card, students write a celebration ("What makes you smarter?") with a point of confusion on the other side ("What do you still hope to learn?"). At the end of the day, each child hands his or her completed card to the teacher, pausing briefly to restate the celebration. This provides a concrete reference to support planning, so make notes as you notice patterns to support instruction.

Personal Daily Reflection Record

Name _____ Week of _____

Day	The most important thing I learned today is	Peer Share
Monday		
Tuesday		
Wednesday		
Thursday		
Friday		

The most important thing I learned this week is
_____

because _____
_____

Personal Pondering Pad

What It Is

The Personal Pondering Pad is a way to meet the needs of many learners during whole-group or small-group time. Before a whole-group discussion, students use the form to reflect more deeply on a topic, through writing or drawing. For students who get anxious sharing in a whole-group setting, this activity allows them to record their own thoughts before sharing. The form can also be used in small-group guided reading activities for students to record their ideas as they wait for peers to finish reading. This offers a management tool that will give you insight to their thinking.

Instructional Focus

writing to support learning, discussion

When to Use It

Introduce the Personal Pondering Pad at the beginning of the year so that it becomes a familiar ritual for any learning experience that will be enhanced by more thinking time. It's a great springboard for kids to activate prior knowledge, respond to or generate a question, initiate a list, or hold their thinking as they participate in a class discussion. It will also provide a concrete tool for teachers to check in on individual student understanding during whole-group instruction or to support discussion after reading.

What to Do

1. Write the word *pondering* on the chalkboard and ask students what comes to mind. Add ideas, such as "to contemplate," "to review," and "to think about"— and even more quirky definitions like "to mull over," "to chew an idea," and so on. Emphasize to students that this form will give them the time and space to be thoughtful as they ponder their own ideas.

2. Ask students the following: Do you tend to like to stop and think before you answer a question? Or do you prefer to offer the first thing that comes to mind? What are the advantages and disadvantages of each? Point out that pondering can be both a place to blurt out first thoughts and a place for thoughtful revision and exploration of ideas.

3. To give students a trial run with the Personal Pondering Pad, conduct a brief read-aloud of three to five minutes. Then model as you answer something you are wondering about, jotting down your thoughts as they occur on the pondering pad. Emphasize that these notes are just brief ideas you want to remember. When students are ready, they can add their own pondering in

continues

Teaching Tips

* Consider printing these forms on bright yellow or pink paper, so that the form itself is a cue to remind students to slow down and reflect.

* In the early grades, you may want to allow students to draw or give them the choice of drawing or writing. Model how each of these are tools to reflect our thinking in meaningful ways.

* Pondering Pad may be used before, during, or after a learning activity. Model how to write key words rather than sentences, emphasizing that attempting to write too much makes it hard to pay attention to the learning. Take time to demonstrate how we use notes to support a discussion by elaborating on these ideas rather than simply reading what is written.

* This activity can also be used in small-group, peer-supported, and independent learning—or any time you want students to think first. It will give slower readers time to finish reading while faster readers can reflect on reading.

* Use Pondering Pads as a spelling tool as students try spelling unfamiliar words, which encourages their independence. This will offer you a revealing glimpse into words that are not yet part of their sight vocabulary to support instructional goals.

* Use the form to brainstorm any ideas for learning at all stages. For example, if you use a poem to highlight words with an -*at* chunk, students may write two examples before reading, add words that were in the poem during reading, and explore new examples after reading.

written or picture form, either alone or with a partner. Rotate as they work to offer support their efforts and offer advice.

4. Encourage students to share their response with a partner or the group. Writing should be in pencil so changes and additions are possible (and welcome). Emphasize that it's not about spelling or being right or wrong, but taking the time to ponder first, and that some need more pondering time than others before sharing orally. This discussion will help students understand their own thinking as they learn to be more respectful of the many differences among learners.

5. Engage students in exploring how the Pondering Pad can be used in a variety of ways when more thoughtful reflections are needed and record their ideas. Make the Pondering Pads readily available for those students who find them helpful to use in *any* learning activity.

Teaching Tips

✱ Use Pondering Pads as a concrete reminder to think before responding. Students can place their hand on the Pondering Pad to signify that they have finished reading or are ready to answer. They may also jot down an idea on the Pondering Pad as they wait.

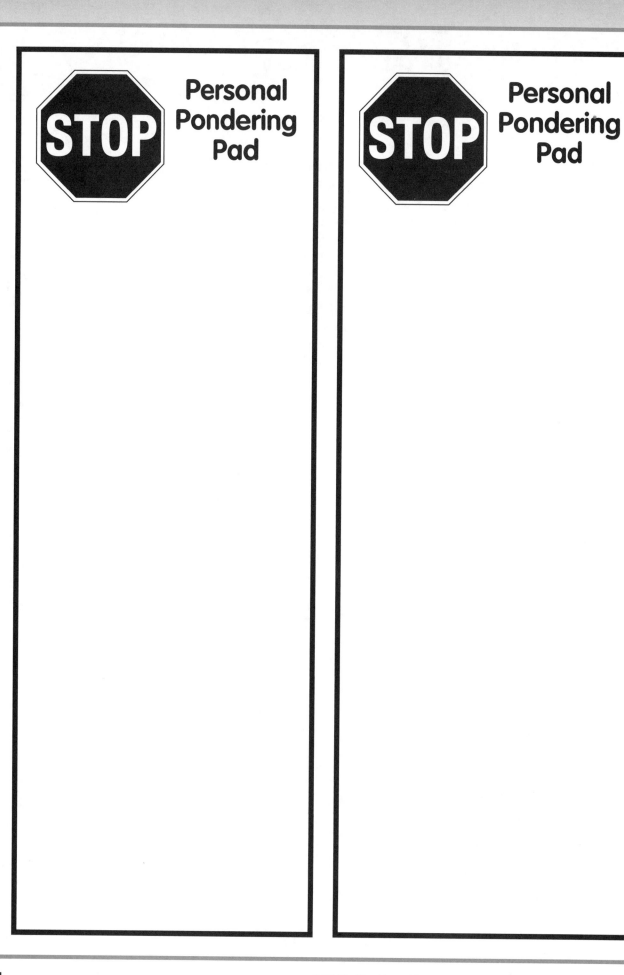

STOP Personal Pondering Pad

STOP Personal Pondering Pad

Making Reading More Purposeful

Frontload Methods

rontloading is a term used in many fields—as it suggests, it means to load up something early in a process. In teaching, we frontload whenever we get students ready for a new learning task or topic by building necessary background knowledge for them to understand the new concept. Often frontloading is associated with a teacher swiftly building background before a book by, say, showing a video clip or reading aloud a short article on the historical period of a novel. In this section, I introduce frontloading activities with a second focus on giving children information that makes their reading more intentional with a clear purpose for reading. The overarching goal is to help children be aware that in addition to reading for pleasure, we read for a variety of purposes, and must adjust the way we interact with texts according to our intentions and the text demands.

The frontload ideas in this section support students before, during, and after reading. Over time, they help kids to see books—or any text—as a vehicle for an enjoyable cycle of reading, thinking, and responding—leading to more thoughtful and engaging reading.

Specifically, the activities here help students set purposes for their reading. They reinforce the idea that we read to understand, but to understand we have to actively make sense of texts, and sometimes the very first step in the process is wondering the following: What do I expect to learn from this text? What do I know about this topic that will help me read this book? What am I curious about? Then, during reading, active engagement in understanding means noticing important details, knowing which details to let go of or hold on to, summarizing, inferring, and so on. These are all important reading strategies we must explicitly teach and continuously reinforce.

Activities at a Glance

Here is a quick reference to the activities you'll find in this section.

Focus Form

Students use a card or form to keep track of a specific purpose and record important details related to that purpose as they read.

> **Setting:** Whole-group and independent work
>
> **Instructional Focus:** *reading, writing about reading*
>
> **Forms:** My Focus Form

Summary Preview

Students get support reading a challenging text by first previewing the text with a brief, teacher-recorded summary. Students then add new details to the summary as they read.

> **Setting:** All settings
>
> **Instructional Focus:** *reading, writing to support learning*
>
> **Forms:** Summary Preview, Summary Preview sidebar strips

Dictionary Redefinition

Students use a formal definition as a springboard to develop a personal definition of a word. Their engagement in word learning helps to ensure students learn the word at a deeper level.

> **Setting:** All settings
>
> **Instructional Focus:** *vocabulary*
>
> **Forms:** My Dictionary Redefinition

Reader's Toolbox

As they read, students track important elements of a text using sticky notes as placeholders. Students can then refer to their sticky notes to write a response according to key categories for discussion and review.

Setting: All settings

Instructional Focus: *reading, writing to support learning*

Forms: Reader's Toolbox Labels, Reader's Toolbox Recording Form

Focus Form

What It Is

A Focus Form allows the teacher to set a specific purpose for reading a text that remains visible throughout reading. The teacher writes the purpose on the form and places it in or near the text. As students read, they can refer to the form to maintain that focus and record important ideas related to the purpose. The form can then be used to support a discussion, during which students evaluate their understanding of the purpose or add new ideas.

Instructional Focus

reading, writing about reading

When to Use It

Focus Forms are reserved for more challenging texts (such as instructional texts) or when students need to read with more purposeful intent, like content area texts or reading for imagery.

What to Do

1. Prepare a Focus Form for students. You can write the focus on the form and distribute it to students in advance, or you may decide on the focus with students after a preview of the text. A focus will depend on the text selection and instructional goals, and may include a question (about character, theme, imagery, or something factual) or invite kids to use a particular strategy (context clues, inferring, visualizing, and so on).

2. To start, model for kids what it means to read for a specific purpose. Make sure they have copies of the text or that you project the text for them to read. Think aloud, stopping at three to four logical points in the selection to discuss what you notice and record key thinking you want to highlight. Students gain from watching and hearing how you discover the places in the text that answer your purpose (whether it's a pivotal moment between characters, a highly sensory description, a key word, an important idea, or the nonfiction fact you were looking for).

3. Then, invite students to practice with the same text or a different text. Guide them to place the Focus Form with the purpose recorded nearby as they read. Circulate and offer support. Pause to ask students if they are keeping the focus in mind as they read. Ask for specific examples in the text, strategies that were helpful, or clues the text provided. Keep doing brief demonstrations for the next few days until you're sure they understand. These continued demonstrations offer tools for increased independence later.

continues

Teaching Tips

* If you teach beginning readers and writers, you may wish to use blank 4-by-6 index cards instead of the form. Many first graders like the extra space to write and draw pictures so this will depend on the students. An index card offers a flexible tool that can be used at any time.

* The Focus Form work well for building children's word knowledge. You can reinforce what you teach in whole-group and small-group lessons by giving students a focus for their independent reading. Students can look for vocabulary, particular spelling patterns, prefixes and suffixes, grammar—the possibilities are limitless. Students then bring their findings back to the class, where they can be added to class reference charts. This makes students responsible for collecting and organizing words.

* Gradually relinquish responsibility to students as they use the Focus form to generate their own purpose for reading. Independent reading will provide an excellent transition for increasing independent use of the form.

Focus Cards *(continued)*

4. On other days, have the students bring their completed Focus Form to a classroom discussion of a book you've all read. Their notes will help them to locate ideas in the text. Encourage students to read specific examples in the text to support their thinking. Students may also add new ideas to their forms that they learn from peers. The Focus Form can also be used to support writing about reading later using details, references, words, and page numbers. Emphasize that the Focus Form will support their thinking as they add new meaning.

5. Students can evaluate their work at the bottom of the form. Encourage them to verbalize their thinking with specific examples so they use this learning or make adjustments in future readings. The discussion that revolves around their evaluation is important, so encourage them to verbalize specific strategies they found useful or why ideas were recorded on the form.

My Focus Form

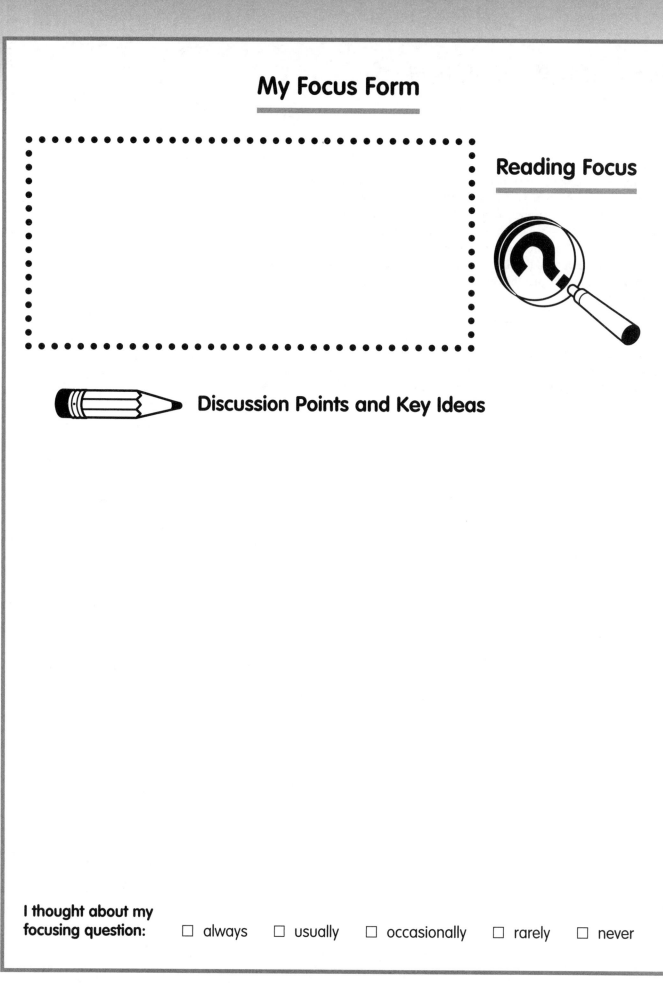

Reading Focus

Discussion Points and Key Ideas

I thought about my
focusing question: ☐ always   ☐ usually   ☐ occasionally   ☐ rarely   ☐ never

Summary Preview

What It Is

A Summary Preview gives students an overview of a text they will read and invites them to provide details that support it using the text as a resource. The summary you provide is generally written at an easy readability level, so that students are given a boost as they take on a challenging text. You can ask children to record details in the sidebar as they read or present it as an after-reading activity, done together or individually, after you have carefully modeled the thinking

Instructional Focus

reading, writing to support learning

When to Use It

This activity is best used either to scaffold students' reading of challenging non-fiction texts or to assist them when more concentrated attention is needed.

What to Do

1. Devise a Summary Preview before reading. You can cast it as a short paragraph, a list, or even as a few questions that hint at the text's main ideas. Remember, what you write should point kids in the right direction of finding pertinent details, but not give them away. For example, the summary may state that there are two kinds of elephants; students would then identify African and Indian elephants and write these findings in the sidebar as this information is located during reading. The summary should highlight key concepts, build anticipation, and set a purpose for reading.

2. *Before reading* a book, ask students to make predictions based on the title and cover. Hand out the Summary Preview to students. They can read it silently or you may read it aloud, depending on the level of student support needed. Encourage them to verbalize what they expect to learn as they read.

3. *During reading*, support students as they read and identify supporting details. Let them know it's preferable to write only key words or sketch visuals. Think aloud your process of determining the important details and condensing this to key words if students need this support, and encourage them to think aloud too. More support will be needed in the beginning.

4. *After reading*, use the form to discuss the text together. Invite children to share their ideas using their notes. The bulleted points recorded in the sidebar offer a brief reference that will encourage elaboration during discussion and sharing. Probe for additional details as appropriate.

Teaching Tips

∗ The form can also be used as a supportive guide for writing since the preview and new details provide a written reference. Demonstrate how to turn these key points into sentences and organized paragraphs.

∗ You can modify the form to initiate writing about a specific topic. Use a teacher read-aloud or shared reading to add details about the topic in the sidebar with students. The details can then be used to write about the topic in the left space. Students may also write a paragraph first, using the bar to record spelling corrections, new word choices, or editing goals identified during a teacher conference.

∗ Individual strips of the sidebar can also be placed directly in any text to add new details during reading. The strips then travel from page to page as new information is added and can be easily removed for sharing. Students then use the strips to review with varied partners and add any new details learned.

∗ Use color-coded strips to identify sections for small groups to read during jigsaw activities or to categorize specific topics of learning. Color-coded strips can also be used to distinguish specific words or patterns. These can then be displayed or combined using a ring holder as a long-term reference.

Summary Preview

Name _____ **Date** _____

Title _____

New
Details
I Learned!

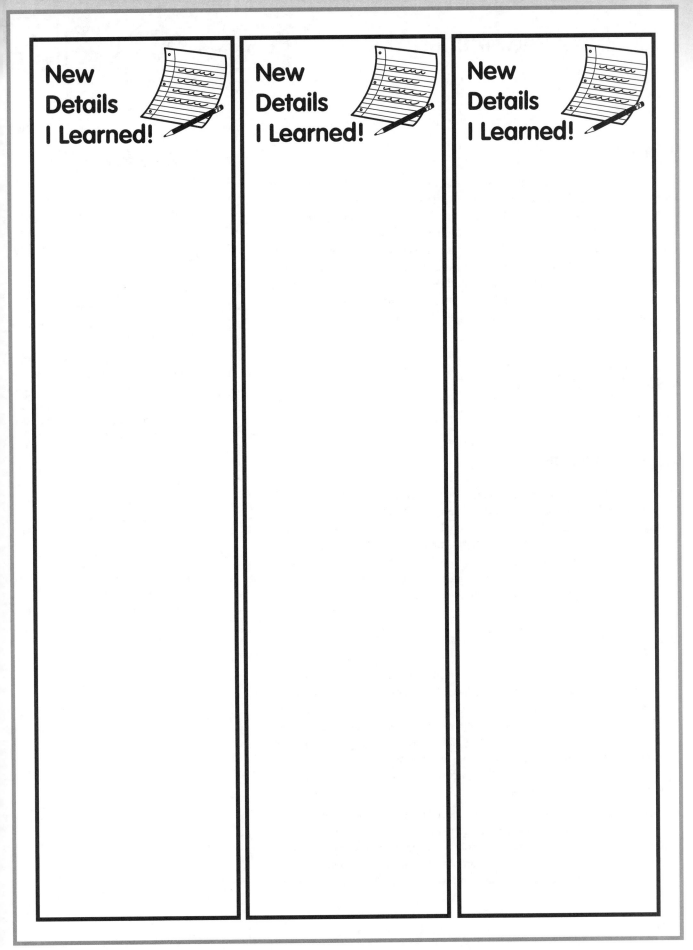

New Details I Learned!	New Details I Learned!	New Details I Learned!

Dictionary Redefinition

What It Is

Dictionary Redefinition teaches students that vocabulary acquisition is more active than looking up a word's definition in the dictionary (and serves as a reminder for teachers). Begin with a dictionary definition to initiate thinking. Students use a "Dictionary Redefinition" form to create a new definition that will reflect their growing understanding. Students make connections between what they know or do not know; they consider varied relationships such as antonyms, synonyms, root words, or patterns; and they add details about the word to place it in a personally meaningful context. As students come across the word in various books or discussions, they can then revisit their ideas and add new knowledge of the word.

Instructional Focus

vocabulary

When to Use It

Use this activity to teach students that learning new words is not a one-shot deal, but occurs over time through multiple encounters with the words—in reading, writing, and talking. Emphasize that vocabulary learning requires exploring words from many viewpoints. The form helps students track their evolving word understandings and provides a forum for vocabulary work that can connect with whole-group, small-group, and one-on-one reading and discussion. It's also ideal for learning the definitions of new content area words.

What to Do

1. Model the activity on the board before introducing the form so children pick up on the thinking process that underlies it. Write a dictionary definition verbatim on the board and read it with students. Discuss and analyze the quality of the definition as you underline helpful words and circle words students do not know. Emphasize that dictionary definitions often refer to other words we may not know, and that this sometimes is okay and sometimes makes it harder to get the meaning. Identify any confusing words that are helpful to know and look them up in the dictionary.

2. Next give an example of the word in context through a reading or learning activity. As you learn more details about the word, engage students in adding (on the board) any terms they feel should be included to make the definition more descriptive or accessible. For example, students may suggest substituting a more familiar term for a confusing word in the dictionary definition.

continues

Teaching Tips

* This activity works extremely well with a small group, as students negotiate a new definition. Students may collaborate at any or all of the stages of the form. For example, students may complete the entire form together or work on their own until they are ready to decide on the redefinition. More support will be needed in creating the redefinition in the early stages.

* Create a classroom visual display with a dictionary definition surrounded by students' new and improved illustrated definitions. This display will help students of different reading abilities gain vocabulary through the power of peer collaboration. The display can then become a class Redefinition Word Book for long-term reference.

* Use the dictionary redefinition card for small-group guided reading. Begin with a dictionary definition of the topic (camouflage). As students read, they can gather details to record in the sidebar. This is an excellent way to offer more targeted support using an appropriate text as students are gaining independence.

When first introducing this activity, work together to move, rearrange, add, or substitute words as you emphasize the thinking process.

3. Students then add an illustration to support the definition. Creating the picture before writing the redefinition will help students think about the word at deeper levels and provide a visual that will support them as they reflect on the new definition. It is important that you verbalize this thinking and encourage students to do the same by drawing a connection between concepts and visual representations.

4. Students will use all available information to write the redefinition at the bottom. Engage them in discussing important points on the form. These may be highlighted for emphasis. The redefinition phase of the activity is the most challenging, so provide teacher support for as long as necessary. In the beginning, you may assume full control by thinking aloud as you create the redefinition (model). Gradually, let students assume increasing control by helping you modify the original sample (shared) or eventually create it with decreasing support (guided), with a peer (partner work) or on their own (independent).

5. When students are ready, they can use the form on their own or with a partner as you rotate to offer support. This will further increase the value of the activity since each pair can share a variation of the redefinition. Discuss the significance of those variations and how each one adds to their understanding. You may then use these combined examples to create a new, shared definition that you post on a class chart.

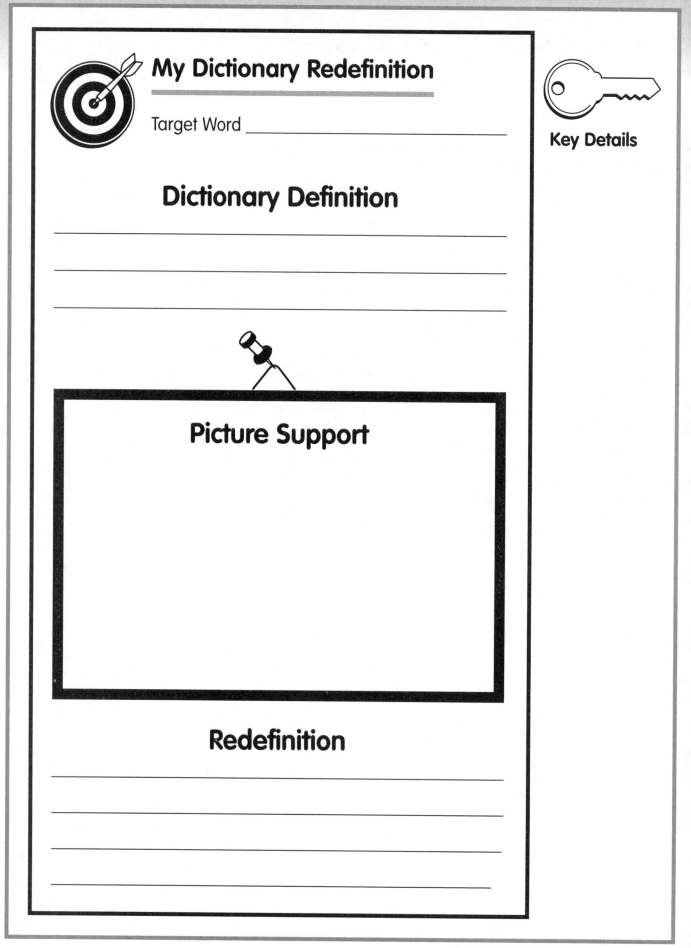

My Dictionary Redefinition

Target Word _____

Key Details

Dictionary Definition

_____

_____

_____

Picture Support

Redefinition

_____

_____

_____

_____

Reader's Toolbox

What It Is

The Reader's Toolbox is an organizational tool to support an active stance as students read. Use sticky notes coded according to color, size, and shape to represent specific elements of a text—character, supporting details, vocabulary, or something that strikes students as important or interesting. As you can see on the diagram on page 48, I've named eight categories and selected varying sizes and colors of sticky notes to represent each one; you can easily adapt these selections to suit your needs or different types of texts. Students use sticky notes to track important aspects of the text as they read and then use the recording form to record notes explaining their thinking. The sticky notes serve as a temporary placeholder while their notes on the form are used for discussion and review. This alleviates the need to constantly replenish sticky notes since they are reusable.

Instructional Focus

reading, writing to support learning

When to Use It

Reader's Toolbox is intended for when you select a very brief section of text (a passage or a few pages) in order to have students focus on something you want them to practice. For example, you could use the activity as a means to have students look for character-revealing details. You could focus on details directly stated or get at it through the lens of teaching students to infer by cluing in on telling details about character actions and dialogue. In other words, you can use the form to demonstrate this thinking and have students practice comprehension strategies using a meaningful context.

What to Do

1. Make toolboxes for your students. Cut folded file folders in thirds horizontally to make three toolboxes from each folder. Glue a label (page 49) to the front of each toolbox and open them vertically to place sticky notes as shown in the diagram (page 48). You can vary suggestions as long as each category has a distinctive size, shape, or color represented by the sticky note.

2. In the early stages of using this activity, move back and forth between modeling and independent practice for several days always using a brief selection. Introduce a text element and verbalize your thinking, explaining why you decided to place a sticky note in a specific part of the text. In the early grades, use shared reading or big books for an extended period and focus on only one category so that you have more time to model the thinking.

Teaching Tips

❋ Create a large poster that gives a visual overview of sticky note categories for student reference as you are explaining each of the categories. Emphasize that they are used as placeholders to revisit later.

❋ Use small-group guided reading to offer more support and teacher modeling over several days. Divide the text into smaller selections and use one category at a time as you find selections and record them on the form. Limit the number of sticky notes so that students learn how to focus their thinking as they read. Ample teacher support will be needed in the early stages.

❋ This activity works well when students make these decisions with a partner. Partners may also work together after independently placing sticky notes to discuss their choices. Foster deeper thinking by encouraging students to justify their decision making and to agree upon the most important selections. This negotiation is a powerful way to revisit the text to justify or modify selections with a partner.

❋ Toolboxes may also be used during independent reading activities with a specific focus, such as

"Find one interesting vocabulary word to investigate and teach."

"Identify two character traits described by the author."

"Find three adjectives you want to use in your own writing."

continues

3. Continue modeling how you use the sticky notes for one category at a time using a text that supports that category. When you have introduced all of the categories, hand out the form to students. The sticky notes serve as a helpful reference to bring the discussion back to specifics of the text or to revisit important concepts or ideas using a concrete tool. The thinking process is particularly important, so encourage students to verbalize why they placed a sticky note in a particular place and to explain the significance of that selection. Students should use bulleted points with key words and visuals to record their ideas on the form or they may note a page number to support discussion later. Support may be needed to help students to condense their notes.

4. After reading, use the form for review and discussion. Students may share important ideas with the group or a partner using the form as a reference. This is a good time to reread key ideas as you encourage students to use the text to support their selections. Remember that the text is always the focus, using sticky notes only to support that text as the tool.

5. After students have gained independence you can extend this to independent reading or partner work. Discussion will be an important part of this application. Periodically, debrief with students in a whole-class setting to discuss how this is a useful strategy. However, some students may not find it as useful and should be allowed to drop it as appropriate.

Visual Overview for Creating Toolboxes

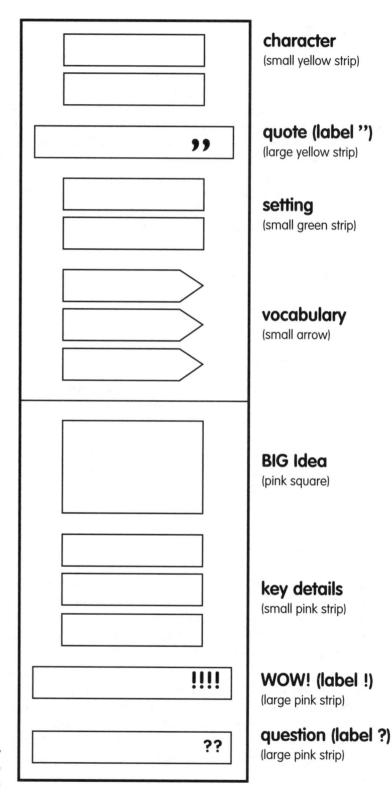

character
(small yellow strip)

quote (label ")
(large yellow strip)

setting
(small green strip)

vocabulary
(small arrow)

BIG Idea
(pink square)

key details
(small pink strip)

WOW! (label !)
(large pink strip)

question (label ?)
(large pink strip)

Reader's Toolbox Recording Form

character

_____

quote ,,

_____

setting

_____

vocabulary

_____

BIG idea

_____

key details

_____

WOW! !!!!

_____

question ??

_____

Promoting Long-Term Word Knowledge

Words in Review

I t's no accident that vocabulary is integrated into many activities in this book. Providing daily opportunities for students to learn a wide variety of words in the authentic contexts of reading, writing, talking, and listening is a boon to kids' literacy. But we also need to offer activities that allow students to take ownership of words by promoting deeper levels of knowledge. Since multiple exposures to unfamiliar words are necessary for acquiring new vocabulary, each of the activities in this chapter is designed to be motivating enough to bear repetition with high engagement.

Fisher and Frey (2008) articulated five big ideas to keep in mind about word learning, taking their cue from the power of the Gradual Release model. While the authors focus on the role of content area words, the same ideas can be applied to any word learning procedure.

1. **Make It Intentional.** Instruction that revolves around words always begins by intentionally selecting the words that are worth teaching and relevant to a topic, learning goal, or the needs of students. Once we make these important decisions, we then must determine the most effective way to teach those words.

2. **Make It Transparent.** Teacher modeling allows us to teach problem-solving procedures and word learning strategies. Whether we are using planned minilessons on prefixes, think-alouds with a textbook, or impromptu wonderings about a word during a read-aloud or a conference, modeling opens windows into our thinking and builds our students' curiosity about words.

3. **Make It Useable.** Students need to take ownership of the words we teach and this can only occur through opportunities to use those words in a variety of learning experiences. Immediately after modeling, students need time to use the words they've been taught in authentic contexts in order to import them into their own vocabulary. Collaborative discussion, reading, and writing tasks give student the opportunities they need to own words for life.

4. **Make It Personal.** It is critical to give students time to independently explore new words and apply the words you've taught as they employ strategies within their own thinking and writing. These opportunities help us build bridges from our instruction to meaningful experiences with words on their own.

5. **Make It a Priority.** Word learning is a schoolwide goal. We must make wide reading a priority in every classroom, with varied opportunities to learn and apply words using high-success texts. This is not about teaching prescribed words in bulk, but teaching a handful of useful words to ensure greater depth of knowledge. Promoting wide reading and collaboration within and across grade levels offers a wealth of experience with words and demonstrates that word learning matters.

Remember that less is more as you prepare for these vocabulary activities. Limit the number of words you teach in order to focus more intensely on those words. By adding peer collaboration and emphasizing the relationships between words, you can increase students' word learning tenfold. Word study that promotes deeper levels of understanding is always time well spent and leads to permanent word learning. This should always be viewed as the end goal.

Activities at a Glance

Here is a quick reference to the activities you'll find in this section

Wearing Words

Students become word experts, capable of teaching their word to peers. Wearing their word on a badge places the word in full view at all times and allows for vocabulary practice at any time during the day.

> **Setting:** Whole-group, small-group collaboration, partner, and independent
>
> **Instructional Focus:** *vocabulary*
>
> **Forms:** Word Expert Cards, Wearing Words Learning Plan

Adopt-a-Word

Each week, students self-select one word from a reading selection that they will learn through repeated use by the end of the week. The combination of choice and repetition leads to more engaged word learning.

> **Setting:** Whole-group, partner, and independent
>
> **Instructional Focus:** *vocabulary*
>
> **Forms:** Adopt-a-Word Learning Record, Adopt-a-Word Record

"Living" Vocabulary

Students plan and pose for a photograph that reinforces a word's meaning to make it more concrete and personal. This is used as a long-term reference.

> **Setting:** Whole-group, small-group collaboration, partner, and independent
>
> **Instructional Focus:** *vocabulary*
>
> **Forms:** "Living" Vocabulary Planning Record

"Code Red" Words

Challenging words are recorded on cards that may include personal definitions, spelling supports, and mnemonic devices, such as a simple trick to remember words or illustrations. These cards are then prominently displayed so that students can easily review the word's meaning and spelling.

Setting: Whole-group, small-group collaboration, partner, and independent

Instructional Focus: *vocabulary, spelling*

Forms: "Code Red" Word Cards, Code Red Word Comparison Form

Stoplight Words

Students identify their level of understanding of words and then build on that understanding by collaborating with peers.

Setting: Whole-group, small-group collaboration, and partner

Instructional Focus: *vocabulary*

Forms: My Stoplight Vocabulary Words, Stoplight Vocabulary Record

Wearing Words

What It Is

In Wearing Words students wear words on badges so that word practice can occur at any time during the day. A weekly reading or learning activity is used to identify a pool of words (generally five). Each student selects one of these words and joins a group that becomes the expert of that word. Throughout the week, students are given opportunities to teach their word and to learn words from other experts.

Instructional Focus

vocabulary

When to Use It

Although introducing the words and preparing to become the expert of a word takes time, sharing requires only minutes. Sharing words is a great transition activity as it is easy to reinforce words in any setting without planning since the card states "Please ask me about my word!" Words are then reinforced throughout the day.

What to Do

1. Introduce a new pool of words each Monday. Select five high-utility words or words that allow you to build on important relationships. These are worthy words that may revolve around quality texts or topics in any content area.

2. Introduce words using a classroom reading activity such as teacher read-aloud or shared reading. Target a specific meaning according to the context of the selection to initiate word study and focus attention on a specific meaning for independent or small-group study.

3. Students select one word for deeper word study and groups are formed based on these selections. Each word expert group will use the form to create a teaching plan by recording key information. Collaboration enhances understanding through deeper engagement with words.

4. Each student needs a Word Expert card placed in a name badge that is worn for the remainder of the week. Each day, students rotate around the room to work with several partners. Students stand face-to-face and share three points:

   Name: "What is the word?"

   Explain: "What does it mean in your words?"

   Claim: "What is a personal, real-life example?"

   Partners restate this learning and add a tally mark on the Wearing Words Plan form to represent frequency of use or multiple exposure to words.

5. During the week, students add a visual reminder of learning to reflect their growing understanding of the words. Encourage visuals with details to reflect this learning. These are used for a sharing activity at the end of the week to further reinforce word knowledge. Repeated exposure to words is key.

Teaching Tips

* After ample modeling, you can modify this activity for independent reading using words that students select. Make sure selections are worthy words that challenge students and that the words' meanings are explained rather than memorized. These personally relevant words lead to high levels of engagement and relinquish control to students.

* Create a bulletin board to highlight learning with a student illustration or make Wearing Word Booklets by adding a personalized definition and picture to the back of the card. These may be added to the wall word cards described in "Code Red Words" on page 63. This will provide continued exposure to previous words to ensure long-term word knowledge while providing an ongoing tool.

* Use Wearing Words to reinforce content area words that revolve around a specific topic. This may require spending more time in the expert groups to explore words from a broader perspective that relates to the topic. Create written references of each word for continued reinforcement such as a display or class-created collection of words related to the topic.

Cards fit into the 2¼-by-3½-inch clip-on plastic badge holders found at most office supply stores.

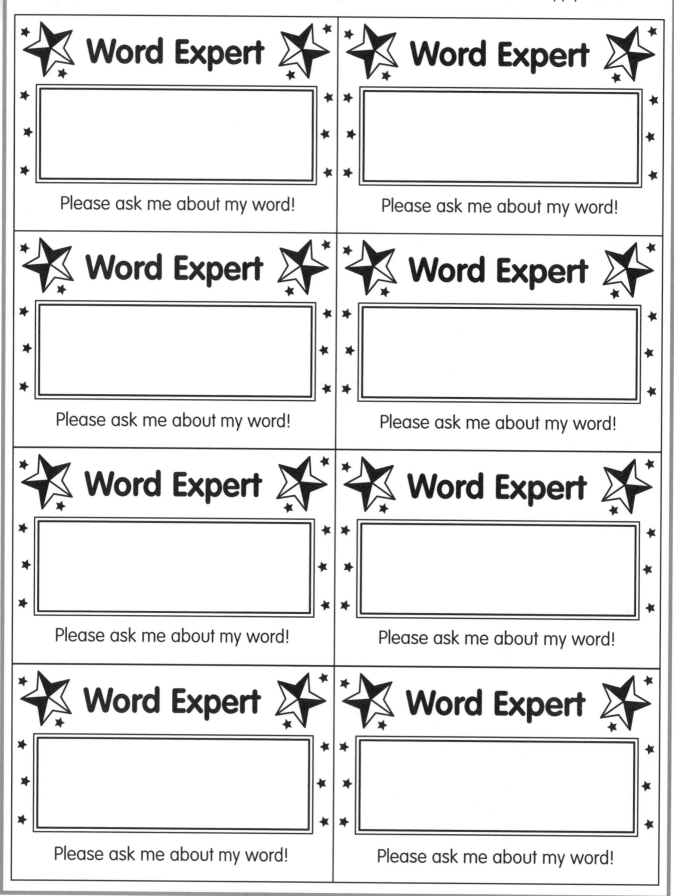

Word Expert

Please ask me about my word!

Word Expert

Please ask me about my word!

Word Expert

Please ask me about my word!

Word Expert

Please ask me about my word!

Word Expert

Please ask me about my word!

Word Expert

Please ask me about my word!

Word Expert

Please ask me about my word!

Word Expert

Please ask me about my word!

Wearing Words Learning Plan

P
L
A
N

Word _____

Word	Learner Tally	Visual Reminder

Adopt-a-Word

What It Is

Adopt-a-Word emphasizes the value of student-selected words and spending time using those words in meaningful ways. Each student adopts one word they are willing to commit to learning by the end of the week. Each day, students will spend time sharing the word with others at school or at home. The form makes it easy to maintain a tally of sharing and gives students a visual reference to promote words in other ways throughout the day.

Instructional Focus

vocabulary

When to Use It

It takes only moments to reinforce words, so this activity can be implemented several times each day in a variety of settings.

What to Do

1. Students select the word on Monday after a shared reading activity; at this time, you should engage students in identifying a pool of words. Using this pool, students will select a word based on the following questions:

   "Are you willing to spend one week with the word?"

   "Is it a word that is worth learning?"

   "Will it challenge you?"

   Continue using the platform of a shared reading to support students for as long as needed, though students eventually can self-select words from other texts. This stage is important to ensure the selection of worthy words and to demonstrate how to prepare for and share words.

2. Each student completes the Adopt-a-Word Learning Record to introduce the adopted word with important details and a student illustration. Students may work independently or adopt a word with a partner. Peer collaboration can significantly enhance word learning at all stages.

3. The goal is for students to use the word as often as they can, recording the frequency of use on their form. Frequency may include working the word into a conversation, noticing it in a book, or using the word in writing. Provide time each day for students to share adopted words with partners by using the words in a conversation or practicing the words on their own. Volunteers may also share words in this way with the group.

4. At the end of the week, each student receives a copy of the word record to show that the word is learned (see page 59). These may be used to review during the year.

Teaching Tips

* Use the word as an instructional extension by challenging students to identify related words. For example,

  "My word is *boat*. Who has a word that begins with the same letter?"

  "We've been talking about how authors use describing words. Who has a word that could be used to describe something?" It would be helpful to keep a list of words for this purpose (see page 154).

* Ensure that students are using the word in thoughtful ways rather than inserting it in a short sentence. Model how to elaborate by adding examples or descriptions and emphasize the value of these details.

* Refer to adopted words during the day as a whole group, with individual students, or in partner activities. For example,

  "What is another word that means the same thing?"

  "What rhymes with your word?"

* Create Adopt-a-Word references such as an Adoption Journal or combine word records with a ring holder to make a review booklet. This can then hang on a wall area designated for this purpose.

* Initiate a cross-grade activity with another group by having students share adopted words across classrooms and grade levels. Any activity that increases exposure to words in meaningful ways will be successful while these experiences model that word learning is a schoolwide priority.

Adopt-a-Word Learning Record

My adopted word _____

My name _____

Circle a number every time you see or use the word

1 2 3 4 5 6 7 8 9 10 11 12 13 14 15 16 17 18 19 20
21 22 23 24 25 26 27 28 29 30 31 32 33 34 35 36 37 38 39 40
41 42 43 44 45 46 47 48 49 50 51 52 53 54 55 56 57 58 59 60
61 62 63 64 65 66 67 68 69 70 71 72 73 74 75 76 77 78 79 80
81 82 83 84 85 86 87 88 89 90 91 92 93 94 95 96 97 98 99 100

Meet My Adopted Word

Adopt-a-Word Record

My name

_____

My adopted word

_____

ADOPT - A - WORD

Adopt-a-Word Record

My name

_____

My adopted word

_____

ADOPT - A - WORD

"Living" Vocabulary

What It Is

In "Living" Vocabulary, students bring words to life by planning and posing for a photograph that will serve as a visual reference of a word's meaning. Each word is introduced in a teacher-supported activity to give students a meaning base. Students then research the word and collaboratively plan how to visually define the word using their own bodies. This plan results in a posed photograph that provides a personalized learning tool to reinforce words.

Instructional Focus

vocabulary

When to Use It

Use this activity to reinforce high-utility, content area vocabulary or other words that come from a variety of resources.

What to Do

1. Introduce the word in a teacher-supported activity, such as read-aloud, to provide a meaningful context for the word. Discuss the meaning using the context in which it occurs, recording an example on the board to highlight that context. Build a basic understanding of the word to support the in-depth study and discussions that follow.

2. Students will then focus on a specific use of the word and investigate to gain deeper understanding. The planning form will help them think about the word, record their thoughts, and plan a photograph to illustrate the meaning visually. This may be done as a group activity in the early grades or with a partner in the later grades.

3. Use this information to create a Living Poster for display on 8½-by-11-inch cardstock. The front of the poster includes the word in large print with the photograph at the top. A second page includes the details recorded on the planning form. These are displayed on the wall for at least two weeks for ongoing review and discussion.

4. Be sure to draw attention to the word during the day for a brief review by asking for related words, real-life examples, or a summary of the meaning. New details may be added to the display as additional information is learned about the words using a variety of resources or learning experiences.

Teaching Tips

* The 8½-by-11-inch cardstock posters make it easy to transfer samples to a three-ring binder or use selected posters in literacy center activities for word extensions. These references provide support and opportunities for review.

* You may initiate posters in small groups using the same word to compare-contrast word variations; alternatively, varied meanings of words may be assigned to different groups.

* The concept of "Living Vocabulary" is easily applied to other learning activities, such as alphabet recognition or word patterns. There is no research to support that the letter *A* must be represented by an apple or that *cat* is the only word that can reflect the rime *–at*. Living Posters allow students to create their own connections using a visual representation in a pose that reflects personal understanding. Posters may also be created to reinforce high-frequency words or visually similar words *(their, there, they're; quite, quiet, quit)*.

* Posed photographs will offer an easy transition to dramatic interpretation. Encourage students to act out words in ways that will reinforce word learning. This will actively engage students with words to further reinforce them.

* Create a "Living Basket" for ongoing review by filling a decorated basket with words written on individual cards. Words are drawn from the basket during the day for students to dramatize for a quick review of words. This continued reinforcement is critical for permanent word learning and allows students to interact with words in a wide variety of ways.

Related Words

_____

_____

_____

_____

_____

_____

_____

_____

_____

_____

"Living" Vocabulary Planning Record

Name _____ Word _____

Dictionary Definition

_____

_____

_____

PERSONAL
DEFINITION

_____

_____

Photograph
Posing Plan

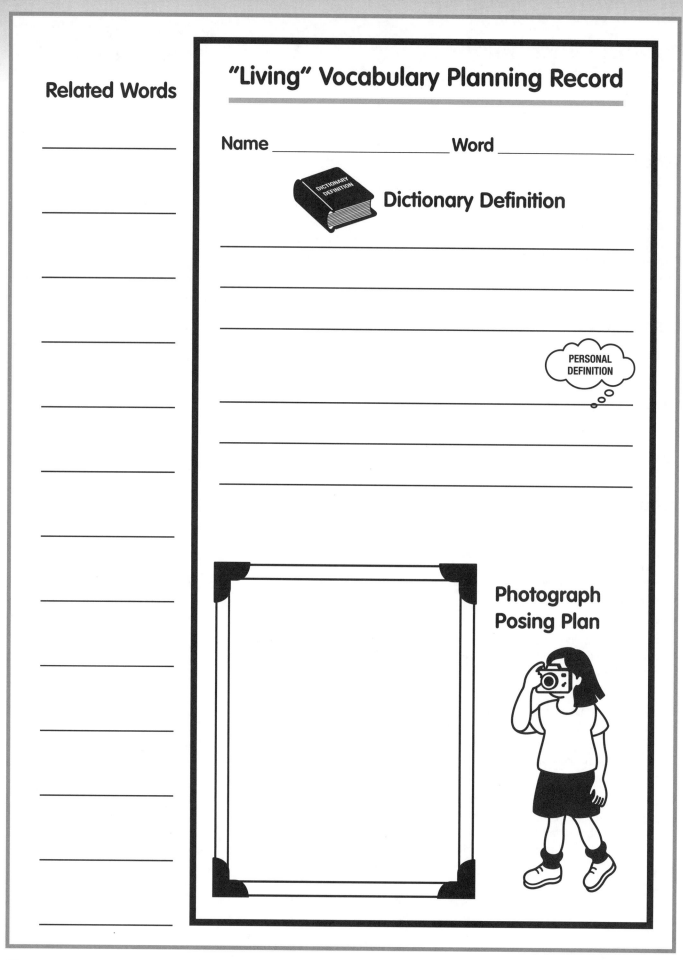

"Code Red" Words

What It Is

"Code Red" describes challenging words that need to be remembered but require more time and effort to do so. In this activity, "Code Red" words are recorded on cards that include group-generated definitions and mnemonic devices, such as illustrations or words that may reflect a confusing spelling. These cards are then prominently displayed in the classroom so that you and your students can revisit these "Code Red" words until everyone is familiar with them. Personal "Code Red" words may also be created for individual students as appropriate

Instructional Focus

vocabulary, spelling

When to Use It

Use this activity prior to a read-aloud or shared text that contains some words that may be challenging, such as sight words *they* or *said*, easily confused spellings, such as *their, they're,* or *there,* or before beginning a topic of study involving difficult words (for example, a lesson on butterflies would contain words such as *metamorphosis* and *pupa*).

What to Do

1. When you first use this activity, explain that "Code Red" is used to describe an emergency. You may create a visual in the form of a stoplight emphasizing that red means to stop and think. Emphasize that these words are very important, yet very difficult, so it is important to spend more time and effort on learning them. The words you and your students identify as "Code Red" words will be displayed around the room to help everyone practice learning them on a daily basis.

2. Introduce these words with examples to reflect learning relevance. Discuss what may make a word "Code Red," such as words that do not fit common patterns or words that have complex meanings or unusual letter combinations.

3. Using the form, demonstrate how to record words on the cards in ways that make them easier to learn. Generate personal definitions, highlight challenging patterns or letter combinations, or add a picture or trick to aid in remembering the word.

4. Display these words around the room in high-visibility spots. Focus on a few words at a time for high engagement and repeated practice. Limit the number of words displayed at a given time to focus more intently on the selected words. Words will change during the year as students change.

continues

Teaching Tips

* Remind students that these words are both a resource for reading, writing, and discussion. Emphasize that using these words in their writing is one way to help them demonstrate understanding and take ownership of words.

* Turn "Code Red" words into a group booklet related to a topic or specific pattern of word learning. These will be used for continuing review and reinforcement.

* Create wall cards for individual sets of words for ongoing practice. Each student will have a set of cards combined with a ring holder or piece of yarn for instant access. Attach cup holder hooks on the wall to hang wall cards for daily practice alone or with a partner or the teacher. Create a second set of cards to reinforce words at home. These can be placed inside a bag for easy transport (dubbed "baggy words" by students).

* This activity can easily be individualized. Use the small cards for student-focused words. Have students identify personal "Code Red" words (or you can help them do so during individualized instruction). Students can then practice these words on their own or with a partner (this partner can be you). The word may also be taped to their desk for immediate access and review as they are learning the word.

"Code Red" Words *(continued)*

5. Take advantage of every opportunity to draw attention to these words and to have students practice them. Students can rotate around the room to practice words or volunteers can spell or define each one from memory. Some words may be highlighted for weeks or months. Pause during the day to highlight one or two words briefly. Spending a few minutes throughout the day will be helpful. Also, use the cards as a reference when words arise in print (Who can find that word displayed on our wall?).

6. Celebrate success by noting when students have integrated these words into their personal vocabulary or can spell them on their own—the words no longer need to labeled "Code Red." Be sure to emphasize that words may need to be recycled to reinforce students' awareness until they become a permanent part of their learning. This often occurs when you remove words too soon or do not reinforce them frequently enough.

Teaching Tips

* Use word cards for a quick review before a small-group activity. Students can share their words with a partner before reading. This is a high-success way to initiate small-group work.

* Let students complete the Code Red Comparison Form with a partner. These may be homonyms, homographs, or easily confused words. Students collaborate to create a visual and "trick" to learn the word for display.

Code Red Word Comparison Form

Name _____ **Date** _____

Code Red Word

Code Red Word

Word 1: _____

How to remember this word

Word 2: _____

How to remember this word

Stoplight Words

What It Is

Stoplight Words helps students reflect on their own level of word knowledge and then offers the support students need to increase that knowledge.

Instructional Focus

vocabulary

When to Use It

Use this activity to help students learn to assess the difficulty of words on their own. Eventually, students will be able to self-monitor as they read and identify words for further study based on their level of difficulty.

What to Do

1. Model this activity in a meaningful context, such as teacher read-aloud or shared reading activities. After a reading or learning activity to establish context, introduce a pool of from three to seven words (select fewer words for the lower grade levels).

2. Ask students to select one word for each stoplight category that reflects their knowledge of that word.

   Go: I can teach this word. *Go* words are words to teach to others, so students commit to learning these words more deeply for sharing purposes.

   Yield: I need to learn more about this word. *Yield* words are partially known, so at least one new detail will be added to enhance understanding.

   Stop: I need someone to teach me this word. *Stop* words are unknown words someone else will teach. Students may work alone or collaboratively on *Go* or *Yield* words, while peers or the teacher will teach the *Stop* word.

3. Remember that awareness of word difficulty is as important a goal of this activity as the process of word study. Circulate among students while asking probing questions that foster discussion about words, such as the following:

   "Which words are more challenging?"

   "Does the author give you any clues as to the word's meaning?"

   "What resources will be helpful to learn more about those words?"

   "How can you help someone understand that familiar word?"

   "What new knowledge do you need to learn more about this word?"

4. Discuss the learning experience at the end of the week to reinforce and extend word knowledge. Encourage students to verbalize their learning experiences or describe how this learning will be applied independently.

Teaching Tips

* Make a stoplight with each of the three categories labeled to display word learning. Use this as a reference to discuss that everyone has different experiences with words and different levels of knowledge and that we can work together to build our knowledge.

* Words may also be reinforced in a literacy center activity as students work with words, using word resources with specific and varied tasks to complete.

* Extend this concept beyond the forms by asking students to reflect on words in other teacher-supported, peer, or independent contexts. Emphasize that many factors can make words harder to learn such as limited prior knowledge, the author's failure to provide a rich context, or lack of personal experiences or exposure to words.

My Stoplight Vocabulary Words

Name _____ **Week of** _____

STOP _____

YIELD _____

GO _____

My Stoplight Vocabulary Words

Name _____ **Week of** _____

STOP _____

YIELD _____

GO _____

Stoplight Vocabulary Record

Name _____ Date _____

Title _____

Study Notes (I learned a new word)

STOP

Share Notes (I added new information)

YIELD

Teach Notes (I will teach this word)

GO

Repetition with a Purpose

Rereading Texts for Accurate Fluent Reading

We want our young readers to read a text with fluency and expressiveness so that the meaning the author has intended comes to life. A fluent reader isn't merely a speedy decoder but someone whose command of words, syntax, and genre structures effortlessly combine so that the child can both understand and *enjoy* the text. A fluent reader knows the distinct voices of characters signaled by dialogue, intuitively slows his pace at important or complex junctures, is moved to tears or laughs in all the right places—all responses that blend the author's words and the reader's background.

There are many strands of teaching that weave into this goal of accurate, fluent reading (Taberski 2009, 2010). Instruction to develop students' automatic word recognition, matching students with just-right books, conducting shared read-alouds often so students develop an ear for what it means to read with expression, inviting children to do choral reading of poetry, increasing students' reading practice with reading buddies—these are just a few of the things we do to develop children's fluency.

In this section I'll focus on rereading as a means to promote comprehension *and* fluency, but with the caution that we keep fluency practice from getting out of hand. There has been a tremendous push for fluency in recent years and while fluency is indeed an important part of reading, it's reckless when it's practiced in isolation and tested using stopwatches. Too many kids today feel like bad readers because they get the daily message that good reading and fast reading are synonymous. These strategies are intended to explore fluency from a broader perspective of meaning, expression, and the joyful translation of words as children breathe life into a printed page.

Fluency affects comprehension, and comprehension affects fluency. When a child reads a book to you with good intonation and phrasing that sounds like natural speech, it often means the child is comprehending the story well. Fluency is a sign of comprehension—but not a sole prerequisite or guarantee that comprehension has taken place.

However, when children are given a book that is not a just-right book, and then asked to reread it again and again to practice fluency—well, that borders on foolishness. Imagine reading a text that is far too challenging. As you attempt to make sense of the text word by word, your frustration mounts. Then, we add insult to injury by asking you to repeat the experience with a timed reading. The assumption is apparently that your understanding will grow with a second reading, but the attempt to read more quickly simply leads to more frustration that adds to your sense of failure. It would be hard to justify this as a good use of time or energy.

The rereading activities in this section were developed with these guidelines in mind.

1. Choose high-interest, memorable texts that reinforce students' current knowledge and interests rather than texts with heavy, new conceptual demands. The material can be slightly challenging, but we don't want children to hit a wall of frustration. Focus on a brief section that will take students less than five minutes to read.

2. Include student-selected texts to increase motivation for repeated reading. While they obviously shouldn't be so predictable or easy that students can read with their eyes closed, familiar texts are fine. This familiarity can be highly supportive, particularly when motivation is high.

3. Emphasize to students that the goal is reading with meaning—not reading fast. Set a clear purpose—for example, "Read this paragraph again to see if there are any clues about that word" or "Read again and make it sound like someone is talking." Be sure that students understand that features of expression such as phrasing or pacing are more important than speed and that good readers adjust rate according to the message or purpose for reading.

4. Help students appreciate that rereading includes strategies that extend beyond fluency. Comprehension is enhanced with repeated

readings as it helps to develop reading stamina, text structure knowledge, vocabulary, background knowledge, and confidence—to name just a few benefits. Rereading deepens understanding of character, plot, and theme as students look at an author's work through different lenses. They can enjoy a story on one reading, study the illustrations on a second reading, and so on. Highlight the reciprocal nature of reading and writing by using books as mentor texts—models for students' writing. This focus will motivate students to reread to mine the books for craft techniques they can use in their own writing.

Activities at a Glance

Here is a quick reference to the activities you'll find in this section.

Five-by-Five Partner Reading

Students choose a selection that they will both read aloud with five partners (to practice fluency) and self-select five words to learn.

>   **Setting:** Partner
>
>   **Instructional Focus:** *reading, discussion, word learning*
>
>   **Forms:** Five-by-Five Partner Reading Record

Read, Listen, and Think

Students practice fluency by reading a brief selection aloud on a tape recorder three times to listen to and evaluate their own performance.

>   **Setting:** Partner and independent
>
>   **Instructional Focus:** *reading, discussion*
>
>   **Forms:** Read, Listen, and Think Card, Repeated Reading Practice Record

My Sharing Bookmark

Students learn how to select meaningful passages to read aloud and discuss or compose with partners.

>   **Setting:** Partner and independent
>
>   **Instructional Focus:** *reading, discussion*
>
>   **Forms:** My Sharing Bookmark

Five-by-Five Partner Reading

What It Is

Five-by-Five Partner Reading is an open-ended record sheet for repeated reading of any self-selected text. Students practice reading for fluency by choosing a brief portion of a text to read aloud with up to five partners and identify five words to practice and learn.

Instructional Focus

Reading, discussion, word learning

When to Use It

This activity can be used as a great follow-up to teacher-supported or independent reading. It can be done on a weekly basis as a reading ritual.

What to Do

1. Model Five-by-Five Partner Reading using a teacher-selected text. After reading, explain why you selected a specific portion for rereading ("I really like this part; This is an important idea"); how to read with expression to make the reading more meaningful ("This is very important; I should read this with emphasis"); how to evaluate your reading ("I can do a better job if I practice this part"); and how to select specific words ("There are some words I need to work on").

2. Demonstrate how to read to a buddy as you sit knee-to-knee with the focus on listening rather than following along. Model how to compliment the reading. Create a chart of compliments with students as an example ("I like the way you used expression," "You did a good job fixing that word.")

3. Explain how to select words to record on the form, emphasizing that these are important words they do not already know. Emphasize that the words they use often in reading and writing are good choices.

4. Begin the reading on a Monday so the students can practice all week. Stretching self-selected reading over five days will maintain motivation and attention and allows students to read with several classmates. Students may select from teacher-supported texts, such as shared or guided reading, or independent texts. Remind them that the selection should be brief, generally one to five minutes of oral reading. Emphasize that selections should not be too difficult (with too many challenging words) or so easy that there is no room for growth. Help students select five sight words or vocabulary words that are worthy words they will commit to learning.

continues

Teaching Tips

✳ You can extend read-aloud or teacher-supported learning activities by creating a collection of texts for oral reading, such as favorite classroom poems or rhymes. You can also find many free and inexpensive scripts for readers' theater on the Internet.

✳ You may use this activity to discuss or assess word learning by completing a quick check of words. Create a weekly ritual for learning words using memory cards. Record the word on one side and a picture, mnemonic device, or definition on the other. These can be stored in a bag for daily practice.

✳ This is an excellent activity for home practice; kids can rehearse with a parent or guardian. It will be helpful to write a brief description of the activity so that you can emphasize the goal of developing more expressive and meaningful readings over simply reading with speed. Give parents a copy of the chart of compliments you created with students so these strategies are reinforced in both settings.

5. Listen to every student by serving as the buddy for one reading each week. This will give you the chance to help any student who needs support and to gather informal assessment data to use for instructional purposes. These non-threatening oral reading contexts will offer valuable discussion opportunities.

6. Each Monday, students should identify the selection of review words to initiate practice of the words during the week. The first reading is completed without an audience and evaluated at the top of the form. Five review words are recorded at the bottom of the form for independent and peer-supported study. Students may record the words on an index card so they can be used throughout the week.

7. The same selection is read to one new partner over the next three days (Tuesday, Wednesday, and Thursday). Each buddy signs the form (Buddy 1, 2, and 3) and offers the reader a compliment. Students will also practice the words alone or with the buddy.

8. A final reading occurs on Friday with the last self-evaluation. This reading may occur alone or with the support of a peer (or teacher). This is also time to assess the success of word learning and determine whether students can read, write, or explain words. This may occur with a partner or the teacher. The word reference may be saved for future review.

Five-by-Five Partner Reading Record

Name _____ Date _____

Text _____ Page _____

My first reading evaluation →

Okay	Good	Great

Buddy 1	Buddy 2	Buddy 3

Okay	Good	Great

My final reading evaluation

✔	I selected these tricky words to learn	I can read	I can write	I can explain
1				
2				
3				
4				
5				

Read, Listen, and Think

What It Is

In Read, Listen, and Think, students tape-record and evaluate a personal reading. The evaluation form provides a concrete reference to discuss with a partner or the teacher later.

Instructional Focus

reading, discussion

When to Use It

This activity may be used as part of the Daily Choice Folder Activities (see page 11) or Weekly Independent Reading Options (see page 15). It may also be used as a daily reading ritual for independent or partner work.

What to Do

1. The focus of this activity is on the quality of reading over speed in order to improve both fluency and meaning. To ensure that students understand this focus, create a chart with students to detail these qualitative features of reading. Make three columns for categories of oral reading excellence: pace (not to be confused with speed), expression, and accuracy. Brainstorm specific criteria under each category to display as a reference. Revisit this criteria often, adding new ideas as students develop greater oral reading proficiency.

2. Each student needs a personal text selection, evaluation form, and access to a recording center. It is preferable to create a standing recording center with a tape recorder and blank cassettes or a computer set up for audio recording. Ten-minute cassettes provide just the right amount of recording time (five minutes per side). The text should be at an instructional or slightly challenging level, or one that students can read with an accuracy rate of 90 to 94 percent. Opt for recent texts from teacher-supported shared or guided reading activities. You will then have identified the hard parts so that you can offer immediate feedback and reinforcement when you work with that student.

3. Students choose one minute of the text and read that selection three times. Let students know that they should focus on expressive and accurate reading rather than speed. After reading the same selection three times back-to-back, the student listens to the recording and evaluates each of the readings by marking the appropriate selection on the form. There is also a place at the bottom for the student to detail any improvements from reading to reading. The oral reading criteria chart you created with students may be used as a reference, but encourage specific text examples ("I reread this part," "I corrected this word," "I raised my voice to show emotion here").

continues

Teaching Tips

✳ Consider demonstrating different levels of reading fluency as well as modeling the kinds of improvements students may see with repeated readings. If students see you demonstrate mistakes and how you correct them, they will feel more confident identifying and correcting those mistakes in their own work. Emphasize that mistakes provide a rich learning opportunity if we pay attention. It is also important to discriminate between those errors that are meaningful substitutions, omissions, and insertions and those that change the meaning, particularly beyond the early grades.

✳ When listening to a child read aloud, analyze their fluency by listening for these facets of fluency: accuracy, automaticity, expression, prosody, and parsing (i.e., the child's ability to break a sentence into appropriate phrase units by correctly attending to the syntax of a sentence; when students parse well, the sentences "shake out" into natural-speech-like phrases). This provides far richer assessment information than all-too common numbers that reflect merely speed.

✳ Use Read, Listen, and Think as a partner reading activity. This will make peers a rich source of feedback based on your models as they learn about fluent reading from each other.

4. Ideally, the student will complete a final reading several days later for additional reinforcement of the text. This will reinforce the selection and demonstrate transfer of learning over a period of time while providing an excellent assessment source for the child and teacher if texts were carefully selected (not too easy or too hard). Students will hear their rise as a successful oral reader. (Note: beyond the early grades, use this more sparingly as silent reading is becoming increasingly emphasized.)

5. Use the Read, Listen, and Think recording for teacher-student conferencing as a concrete measurement of oral reading. Although it is not realistic to listen to every recording each week, you can easily target one recording by each student monthly. Highlight five to seven recordings weekly for independent conferencing. Listen to the readings *with* the student, discuss improvements, and add your own observations. Be positive, perhaps making a suggestion or setting a future goal with the student. Use specific examples in the reading to provide feedback or make suggestions, stopping the tape at key points to illustrate specific oral reading samples.

Read, Listen, and Think

Name _____ Date _____

	Poor	Good	Great
Read 1			
Read 2			
Read 3			

I am proud of these improvements

Read, Listen, and Think

Name _____ Date _____

	Poor	Good	Great
Read 1			
Read 2			
Read 3			

I am proud of these improvements

Repeated Reading Practice Record

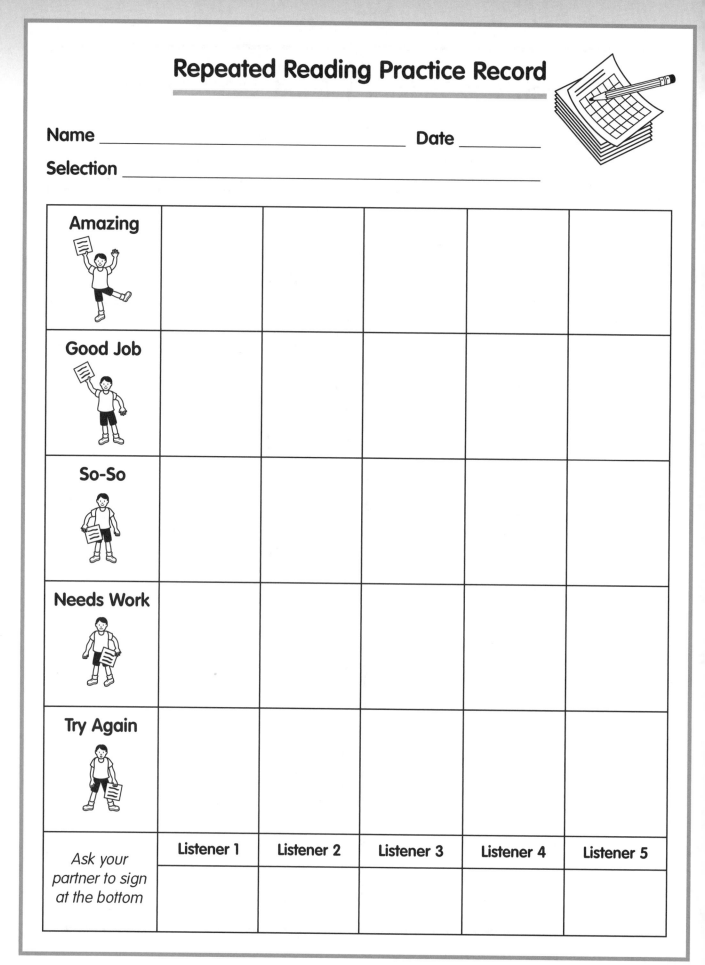

Name _____ Date _____

Selection _____

Amazing					
Good Job					
So-So					
Needs Work					
Try Again					
Ask your partner to sign at the bottom	Listener 1	Listener 2	Listener 3	Listener 4	Listener 5

My Sharing Bookmark

What It Is

My Sharing Bookmark makes it easy to use any text selection for repeated practice. Students learn to choose a selection for reading aloud that fits at least one of three categories: *important*, *challenging,* and *memorable*. Students then practice reading the selection alone or with the teacher before sharing with others to provide engaging discussions and exposure to a variety of texts.

Instructional Focus

reading, discussion

When to Use It

This activity can be used both with independent and shared reading to promote meaningful oral reading and engaging peer discussions.

What to Do

1. Introduce the bookmark by writing the three categories on the board and discussing the meaning as it relates to reading.

   Important: relevant to a topic or a story line

   Challenging: words and concepts I need to explore further

   Memorable: worthy of discussing with others or remembering

2. Modeling is important, which means that teacher read-aloud or personal reading is a good starting point as you can use this to think aloud. Demonstrate how to match the category to a relevant text selection. Verbalize your thinking as you explain your selections and demonstrate how to practice reading orally with expression and meaning.

3. Engage students in the selection process using a shared reading. In the beginning, set a purpose for the bookmark. For example, "As we read today, think about memorable language/words." After reading, students will suggest where to place a bookmark in the text. Vary categories using key purposes for reading and word study. For example, "Today, we'll use the bookmark to find facts that are important to our topic" or "As you read, think about challenging words we need to investigate."

4. The teacher or student volunteers then read brief selections orally for discussion and exploration. Remind students to read with expression so that the text is more meaningful to the listener. Demonstrate how we may read the selection two or three times before reading with a partner while emphasizing that the focus is on getting the message across.

continues

Teaching Tips

✳ Invite students to draw a picture and summarize the reading on the back as an extension activity for a specific text. These can then be displayed as reading samples. This will be a wonderful source of comparison when students have selected from a common text or topic. Or you can ask students to personalize them with color and drawings, and place them in a basket for review.

✳ Try a tape-recorded reading with "Read, Listen, and Think" (see page 77) for additional practice. This is an excellent opportunity to practice a reading before sharing with a partner.

✳ Create a learning display to highlight a specific teaching point or topic that revolves around the bookmarks. For example, you may ask students to find memorable descriptions of a setting or important facts about sharks. These references may also support written summaries or descriptions. Remember that sharing and discussion is an important facet of this activity, so always build in time to reflect on the learning experience.

My Sharing Bookmark *(continued)*

5. After you have provided several demonstrations and modeled the thinking, students can then use the bookmark as they read a text alone or with a partner. Begin with a specific focus (e.g., find a selection that is memorable), but eventually allow students to select their own category and matching text. Students should identify an appropriate selection in the reading to bookmark and practice the reading before sharing it with a partner.

6. Students can then share with a partner by identifying why a selection was made, reading with expression, and discussing the category or instructional focus. You can gather rich assessment by rotating to observe as students work together. As appropriate, ask questions about the reading or suggest discussion points for partners. This will be particularly helpful in the beginning

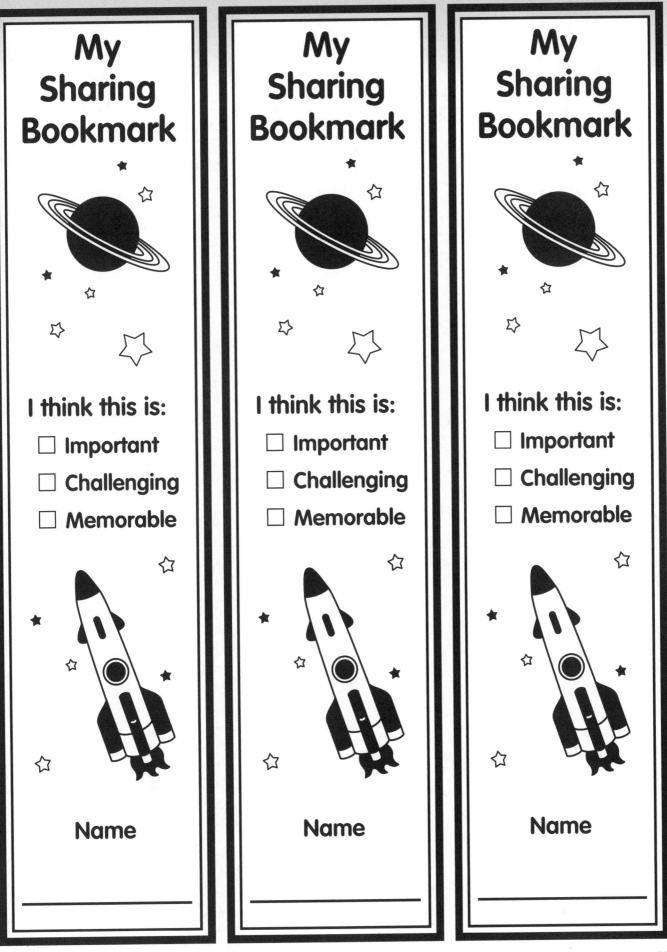

My
Sharing
Bookmark

I think this is:
☐ Important
☐ Challenging
☐ Memorable

Name

My
Sharing
Bookmark

I think this is:
☐ Important
☐ Challenging
☐ Memorable

Name

My
Sharing
Bookmark

I think this is:
☐ Important
☐ Challenging
☐ Memorable

Name

Using Peer Collaboration to Foster Independence

Jigsaw Learning

Jigsaw learning is a cooperative approach that is especially powerful in cultivating a student's sense of themselves as an "expert." As in the interlocking pieces of a jigsaw puzzle, the whole of a learning activity is divided into pieces that are assigned to individual students or small groups. Students assume responsibility for their piece, and become experts who possess the depth of understanding to teach their peers. Ultimately, everyone gains the big understandings of the task and is a valued member of the learning community.

Jigsaw learning is a good illustration of the adage "less is more." For schools implementing RTI (or any school) we need to build in the time necessary for students to achieve success, which is the right of every learner. The activities in this chapter show how to break learning tasks into smaller segments and how to devote more time for the practice students need to become literacy "experts" as they assume more control for their own learning.

Activities at a Glance

Here is a quick reference to the activities you'll find in this section.

Vocabulary Jigsaw

Over the course of a week, students work alone or through collaboration with peers to become word experts and teach their word to others.

Setting: All settings

Instructional Focus: *vocabulary*

Forms: Classroom Jigsaw Vocabulary, Jigsaw Cards

Jigsaw Texts

Students develop their reading to learn skills by becoming an expert of one section of a common content area text topic through note-taking that will be used to teach peers.

Setting: Whole-group, small-group collaboration, and partner work

Instructional Focus: *reading, writing to support learning*

Forms: Jigsaw Text Notes

Jigsaw Poetry

Students read and practice a high-interest poem to build fluency and focus on a target skill by becoming experts of a brief section of the poem.

Setting: Whole-group, small-group collaboration, and partner work

Instructional Focus: *reading, writing about reading*

Forms: Jigsaw Poetry Reading

Vocabulary Jigsaw

What It Is

Vocabulary Jigsaw is a weekly ritual in which students acquire new vocabulary through activities in whole-group, small-group, and partner settings. The teacher introduces words, generally using a whole-group read-aloud, and then students work together in small groups to become the expert of one word. They are then responsible for teaching that word to their peers. Each setting reinforces and builds students' understanding of new vocabulary so they will develop a deeper knowledge of words.

Instructional Focus

vocabulary

When to Use It

Use Vocabulary Jigsaw to develop word learning and memory techniques across the curriculum. You will need to devote a full week to the activity so students have the time necessary to become the expert and teach peers.

What to Do

1. Prepare the jigsaw cards provided by making copies of the form on page 90. Write the number "1" within the boxes on one page, then do the same for numbers 2 through 5 on the additional pages. Print each numbered page on different colored paper. Cards are sized to insert into a name badge.

2. Introduce five words on Monday using a brief text that provides some context to the word's meaning. These words should be content area or high-utility words that demonstrate important word relationships. After reading the context, develop explanations of the words, rather than definitions. These are general concepts so students can explore words in greater detail in the next steps.

3. List the words on the board with an assigned jigsaw number by each one. All students have been exposed to words using a story context so briefly review words and distribute jigsaw cards to form groups.

4. Identify expert categories to record on the left of the form, such as dictionary definition, personal definition, related words (synonyms, antonyms, pattern words, root words), examples (book or real life), and illustrations. Select relevant categories that can be used all year. These categories will vary according to your instructional goals and student needs, but it is best to select categories that will be used all year.

continues

Teaching Tips

✱ Create review cards for ongoing learning. Record key points on individual index cards with a word on one side and important learning concepts on the other, using color-coded cards to identify different content areas. Each set of cards can be put on a ring holder and displayed on a hook as vocabulary wall cards. These can then be used for literacy center activities or independent and partner review or extension.

✱ Write each word on an index card and place them in a Vocabulary Memory Basket. At any point during the day, a student can reach into the basket and withdraw one word for a spontaneous word review. This ongoing review is essential for long-term knowledge.

✱ The completed forms will be a wonderful resource for ongoing review. Students may place the forms in a personal vocabulary notebook and revisit selected words from time to time. Periodically students may have a personal choice teaching day using any of the words.

Vocabulary Jigsaw *(continued)*

5. Students use these categories in collaborative work to become the expert of the assigned word. Students then develop a plan to teach the word to their peers. As students work, rotate among them in order to reinforce or support their efforts. Ask probing questions that allow students to maintain control while modeling how to provide relevant details and supportive visuals.

6. When the expert teaching plan is completed, students rotate to teach the word to one new partner each remaining day of the week. Experts will teach on their own rather than as a group. Peers will stand face-to-face as the expert explains, rather than defines, the word. Encourage students to use all sources of communication, including nonverbal. Partners summarize learning and record this in their own words or list a few key details, reviewing the essential points about that new word. Emphasize that the learning boxes are smaller because their job is to translate learning rather than copy information. This will be important modeling in the early stages.

7. Repetition and review is an important feature built into the activity because forms are stretched across one week. Each student will teach their expert word to a new partner every day for the remainder of the week and then learn one more word. Since students explain rather than read the word meaning, they will adjust their teaching with each new partner.

Teaching Tips

✳ Jigsaw groups may work together to create a word poster using the expert information to display on a vocabulary wall for at least one week. Forms are then placed in a Classroom Jigsaw Notebook with posters collected in a Big Book of Words. These ongoing references provide critical reinforcement.

Classroom Jigsaw Vocabulary

Name _____   Title/Topic _____

	Learning Word:
WORD My Expert Word	
	Learning Word:
	Learning Word:
	Learning Word:

Cards fit into the 2¼-by-3½-inch clip-on plastic badge holders found at most office supply stores.

Jigsaw Texts

What It Is

In Jigsaw Texts, a student will learn about a common topic. The topic will then be divided into key sections so that small groups can work collaboratively to read a specific subtopic and identify key information. In this way, students learn the study skill of selecting and recording key concepts for review as they support each other through peer teaching.

Instructional Focus

reading, writing to support learning

When to Use It

When reading content area texts, use this activity to support students' determining key details and concepts and recording this information in written form.

What to Do

1. As always, modeling is key, and you'll want to do it over several days. Use a teacher read-aloud to introduce the topic, identify a purpose for reading, and demonstrate how you identify the key ideas of a paragraph or passage. Think aloud so students benefit from hearing how you decide which details are minor and can be in effect "set aside"—and which details carry the big idea of the paragraph. Some students will need continued support understanding this critical skill.

2. Model how you record the ideas as brief, bulleted points, including any visuals to support the information. This modeling is important for when students work on their own and use these points for teaching.

3. Assign jigsaw groups and distribute the jigsaw cards, forms, and content area texts. Select three- or four-part jigsaws on pages 93–94. These should be brief selections so that the majority of time can be spent on discussion, note-taking, and peer teaching. Choose categories that revolve around a specific topic such as different types of spiders or character traits. Key portions of text can be assigned, or you may write a brief overview for each group. List on chart paper any strategies you used in your demonstration and think-aloud for students to refer to—author's headings, use of italics, the first sentence of a paragraph, phrases like "in contrast," and so on.

4. Small groups read the assigned text in any way they choose with a specific goal in mind—such as "Identify four key facts" or "Select five describing words." It is helpful to incorporate collaboration and self-selection. For example, "Select three facts as a group and one you personally consider important."

continues

Teaching Tips

* Since the goal is both reading with meaning and promoting long-term recall, it is important to provide additional opportunities to reinforce this learning. Turn student-recorded notes into a display of learning points around the room. Each group can be responsible for recording key learning points on an index card or full-page sheet. Place other books on the topic at varying reading levels in the center. Students can then research the topic independently or with a peer, using other text resources to add new details.

* The key points listed on the form can be used to write a paragraph to summarize the concepts students have selected. These brief points will help students move to bigger, more detailed ideas. This is important teacher modeling in the beginning.

* Each group can create a poster to give an overview of learning points. These posters should be displayed so that students can review learning, teach important points, or add details as a result of new learning activities.

* Modify the activity using Four Corners by placing a poster in each corner of the room. Groups add their learning points to the poster and use this to teach concepts as a group rather than individually.

Jigsaw Texts *(continued)*

5. After reading, students will discuss the text and complete the form together. Remind them to discuss how to record the ideas as bulleted points using key words and visuals to support the information. The teacher should rotate to ask questions, reinforce student efforts, or probe for new thinking.

6. After students have completed their forms, they will teach the information to a partner in another group. You can allow students to teach one-on-one or form groups that include one expert from each Jigsaw Text selection. Experts teach the information by elaborating on the bulleted points and then learners will record the key ideas in their own words on the form. Emphasize that the teacher-learner role is far more than a copying task. The teacher's job is to make the information understandable and respond to any questions while the listener's role is to listen with purposeful intent, ask relevant questions, and interpret new learning on the form.

7. Consider modeling an ongoing process as you review learning and support new thinking with increasingly complex texts or tasks. This is learning that will be essential in the future so it is time well spent. (Also, use this time to add to the list of strategies described in Point 3.)

Jigsaw Text Notes

Jigsaw 1

☐ Teacher
☐ Learner

Topic _____

Jigsaw 2

☐ Teacher
☐ Learner

Topic _____

Jigsaw 3

☐ Teacher
☐ Learner

Topic _____

Jigsaw Text Notes

Jigsaw 1	**Topic** _____
☐ Teacher ☐ Learner	

Jigsaw 2	**Topic** _____
☐ Teacher ☐ Learner	

Jigsaw 3	**Topic** _____
☐ Teacher ☐ Learner	

Jigsaw 4	**Topic** _____
☐ Teacher ☐ Learner	

Jigsaw Poetry

What It Is

Short poems are ideal for repeated readings. Jigsaw poetry applies the jigsaw approach to poems. Each group is assigned an expert role to promote phonics, fluency, and vocabulary. The poems chosen are selected by interest, without the stigma of the label of reading level. Poetry offers an unlimited supply of pleasurable reading.

Instructional Focus

reading, writing about reading

When to Use It

Use Jigsaw Poetry on a weekly basis to develop students' understanding of poetry, fluency, and language conventions such as imagery.

What to Do

1. Introduce a new poem every Monday. Record the poem on a large chart. You will also need 8½-by-11-inch copies of the poem so students will have a large poetry collection by the end of the year. This will be used for repeated practice. Divide the poem into smaller sections and print each section on color-coded strips. Identify one instructional focus such as word choice, vocabulary, rhyming words, use of metaphor, and so on.

2. Use a shared reading activity to introduce the poem. Work out the meaning collaboratively, taking time to identify the poem's message and appreciate the poet's language.

3. After engaging students in shared reading, discuss with students the selected instructional focus using the poem to highlight for examples. Or you could choose to do a brief minilesson where you use the poem to think aloud what you notice about a feature you are highlighting. You want to explore just a little—so students are left with plenty to discover on their own.

4. Form small groups using an assigned portion (line or stanza) on which to be "expert." Groups work together to create a smooth, fluent reading of their section and to explore the assigned instructional focus. The open-ended form provides room for students to record a definition or examples of the instructional focus at the top (learning focus) with a place to summarize the assigned reading in print and with an illustration.

5. Provide time during the week for students to share learning or reread with a partner by rotating around the room. Students may also continue to work in their small group to develop the instructional focus such as to brainstorm a list of related words, record a definition, or explain a concept.

6. Friday is "Hollywood Day," designated for an expressive dramatic reading. Students stand side-by-side in their expert group to take turns completing their jigsaw portion. Each group will try to provide the most expressive rendition.

Teaching Tips

* Display the forms with the poem and create Personal Poetry Notebooks with a copy of each poem (include nursery rhymes and popular songs) for continued practice. This is an excellent resource for daily independent or buddy reading activities, and cross-grade reading partners. Create a second collection for home reading, suggesting daily activity rituals for parents to complete for each poem (Monday: reread, Tuesday: word study, etc.). This is particularly important for students who need more repetition.

* Display the poem in a literacy center with an extension activity to support and reinforce your learning goals (add an example, create an illustration, listen or read on tape). This will provide additional practice that is needed.

* Reinforce the instructional focus by creating a chart to be used as an ongoing reference. Begin the chart on Monday, using the teacher example and adding new student samples during the week. This will allow you to focus on specific instructional points while maintaining the focus on meaningful reading while you are engaging students in creating a long-term resource.

* Students will also enjoy creating "Body Words" by selecting one interesting word in the poem and working together to create a physical movement with a personal definition to teach others. Take a photograph of the body sign with the word and explanation to display around the room.

Jigsaw Poetry Reading

Title _____ **Expert #** _____

Learning Focus

Summary _____

_____

_____

_____

Illustration

SECTION

8

Building Meaning

Engaging Discussion

R eaders quite naturally talk about what they read with others. Even a kindergartner can drive a picture book to the best-seller list with their talk: the word-of-mouth, gotta-have-it about a book is potent stuff. From *James and the Giant Peach* to James Joyce, we love a good story and we love to have others help us clarify understandings about a text or to share our heartfelt responses with them. Reading is social, no doubt about it, and yet we don't make the most of this aspect of it at school. High-level discussions about texts in whole-group, small-group, and one-on-one settings need to be a bigger part of every school day. Discussion-based instruction has been shown to increase the achievement of students of all ability levels. Discussion creates opportunities to revisit past learning and to build connections between ideas and across texts.

In this section, you will find discussion activities that give authentic talk about texts a specific focus. The overarching purpose of these activities is to support students as they are learning how to have rich conversations about books. Thoughtful, exploratory, and productive discussions don't just happen. They take time and training, teacher modeling, sometimes student-negotiated criteria and topics, explicit standards for respectful listening, and meaningful responses. Whole-group modeling and teacher guiding of reading strategies and discussion behaviors will be essential before breaking into smaller groups. Students will eventually participate in student-led book discussions without you, but this can take months of hard work as they collaborate in the knitting together of ideas with support.

Activities at a Glance

Here is a quick reference to the activities you'll find in this section.

Discussion Prompts

Students select from several categories and use this to initiate a discussion with peers that revolves around a variety of high-interest texts.

Setting: Whole-group, small-group collaboration, and partner work

Instructional Focus: *discussion, writing to support learning, reading*

Forms: Discussion Bookmarks, Discussion Prompt Cards, Discussion Prompt Reading Samples

Comprehension Gestures

Students use hand gestures to label a comprehension process they are using during discussion activities. Each gesture represents the thinking process.

Setting: Whole-group and partner work

Instructional Focus: *discussion, writing to support learning*

Forms: Thinking Signs Memory Folder (Labels), Comprehension Gestures Overview Strips, Visual Overview of Comprehension Gestures, Comprehension Gestures Planning Form

Reading Strategy Bookmark

Students practice reading strategies recorded on a bookmark and identify text examples for discussion. This highlights strategies within authentic reading contexts.

Setting: All settings

Instructional Focus: *reading, writing about reading, discussion*

Forms: Reading Strategy Bookmarks, Mini-Bookmarks, My Reading Strategy Examples, Reading Strategy Strips

Discussion Prompts

What It Is

Discussion Prompt cards can help readers actively engage in the text as they read by giving them specific aspects of a story or nonfiction text to notice and talk about. For example, if you look at the discussion points on pages 100–02, students might talk about something that is memorable, confusing, surprising, interesting, beautiful, and so on. In another light, these prompts nudge kids to monitor their comprehension and to share their thinking with peers. You can also laminate these cards or bookmarks and tuck them in books to signal they are ideas ripe for partner and small-group discussions (I call them "sharing categories"). Students can also use the form to write about the text they've read *before* they discuss it. Several variations of prompts are provided to give you flexibility.

Instructional Focus

discussion, writing to support learning, reading

When to Use It

Use this activity to help you introduce the elements of a productive exchange of ideas about a text and the kinds of things engaged readers notice about a text to help them understand and appreciate it.

What to Do

1. Introduce the discussion bookmark topics using a teacher read-aloud to model the thinking for each one. It is preferable to focus on only one topic at a time, moving on to the next one on another day so the discussion is more focused. You may use the individual discussion prompt cards for this purpose or point to the selected topic on the bookmark.

2. Introduce a topic with a specific text example: "I think there was something surprising in this section. It was surprising that ___." Explain why the example was selected and describe the selection in your own words. Use this as the basis for a brief discussion of the text, encouraging students to add new ideas.

3. Quickly make the transition from teacher modeling to student application. A shared reading text is a great way to start. After reading, students sit knee-to-knee with a partner. Each student takes turns identifying the category with a text sample and explanation. Partners are encouraged to ask questions or probe for more information. Remind students to read the sample aloud to support the discussion.

4. When all sharing categories are introduced, use the bookmark in a variety of reading activities. Discussion Prompt Cards may be inserted directly in the text

continues

Teaching Tips

* This activity provides rich assessment information for one-on-one conferring with students. The form may also be used with students during one-on-one or small-group activities. Model the thinking and demonstrate how to put these points in written and visual form. Some students will need more modeling before they can do it on their own.

* Any of the topics can be used to make a display based on a single text or varied selections—and focusing on one topic such as beautiful phrases, interesting character traits, or important words about sea turtles. This is a wonderful way to reflect on varied ways of thinking about books and topics.

* When students are ready, gradually make the transition to partner and independent contexts. Students may complete a form together using a common text or share a completed form using a personal selection. The categories are designed to promote discussion even when students are reading different texts. This is an excellent way to highlight the many ways authors reflect these varied thinking points.

* Periodically, debrief with students to ensure emphasis on using categories for meaningful discussions and written responses. You may create discussion strategy charts with students to reflect this thinking during the year.

as a reference for later writing and/or discussion. In the beginning, you may identify a topic, but gradually allow students to select their own topics and samples.

5. Use the Discussion Prompt Reading Samples form (page 105) when you want students to put their ideas in writing before they share them with peers. They simply identify the topic by checking the box on the left and then add a description or illustration on the far right of the form. The completed form can then be used to support discussions and new points may be added.

Discussion Points for Fiction and Nonfiction

Use the descriptions below to guide a discussion with students so they understand each point. Demonstrate how you notice or tackle each of these things as a reader, doing as much text mentoring or as many read-aloud minilessons as you need until students can pick up on these things in their independent reading. Emphasize to students that talking about and recording what catches their attention will help them understand the text.

Memorable: What is memorable in a text? In fiction, a memorable passage might be an important scene in a story or a smaller moment or even a unique word choice that struck a student. In nonfiction, the student might notice concepts that seem worthy of remembering, or an element of author craft that made the subject easier to understand.

> **⋯⋯➤ *Tips for talking about it***
>
> There are no right and wrong answers here! Students should be ready to point to the place in the text that was memorable to them, share their reasoning for selecting it, and draw out peers' ideas as to what makes it stand out. Respect the personal nature of this category

Confusing: Even the best readers get confused. Sometimes comprehension goes off track because a reader's thoughts wander, sometimes the author hasn't explained something well, and at other times there is a concept or key word that is more challenging or above the head of the reader. The important thing is for readers to notice when their understanding or engagement is shaky, and go back and repair it. Noticing and discussing the confusing parts reinforces this notion that it is up to the reader to be aware when meaning goes off track and to make the effort to clarify understandings.

> **⋯⋯➤ *Tips for talking about it***
>
> It helps young readers to try to pinpoint what exactly made the text confusing. Peers can weigh in on whether it threw them, too, and which reading strategies or actions were helpful to correct that confusion. Emphasize that confusions will vary and that different strategies are useful in different situations for different readers.

Discussion Prompts *(continued)*

Interesting: Interesting, surprising, and important—most of these categories presuppose students are reading high-quality texts! Interesting events or facts are just that—moments in the text that caught the reader's eye on a personal level. They might be noteworthy because they foreshadow a big event or raise an issue of particular interest to a student.

⤑ *Tips for talking about it*

As always, encourage students to freely turn back to the text, reading it aloud for peers, and openly sharing their reasons for noticing a particular detail. Peer contributions will enrich understandings—and over time, readers come to see how no text is experienced in quite the same way by two readers.

Surprising: Wow! I didn't know that! Or, I didn't see that coming! The points in a text when a reader sits up and takes notice are sometimes because the author deftly led you to this moment of surprise. Other times, a reader's surprise is because the author didn't sufficiently foreground the event or the movement between topics.

⤑ *Tips for talking about it*

Discuss how the author can set up readers for a surprise as well as to understand the notion of a fallible author. That is, sometimes when they are confused or surprised, it's because the text's author didn't do a good job of making their ideas clear. Guide students to see how authors lead us to a surprise or when it was the author "at fault" for the surprise. (For more on reading lessons based on author fallibility, see *Improving Comprehension with Questioning the Author* (Beck and McKeown 2006.)

Important: It takes many months and years as a reader to feel sure-footed about determining the significant events or details in a text. Sometimes a text can be so full of interesting facts, it's no wonder readers struggle to point to "the big idea" of a passage or chapter. Yet this is an important reading skill that must be explicitly taught and nurtured.

⤑ *Tips for talking about it*

Use the group discussion to get across the idea that important moments in a text might be a climactic event—when a character's problem is fully revealed or resolved—or it might be a point that is significant because it's the "tipping point" that sets many even bigger plot events in motion (for example, the mother leaves, the dog is lost, the protagonist loses something). In nonfiction, students determine important ideas by noticing how often smaller details explain or support some bigger claim in a paragraph.

Discussion Prompts *(continued)*

Beautiful: Lovely language abounds in both fiction and nonfiction trade books these days. Book-based minilessons that name and illuminate some of the qualities of pleasing prose can give kids an eye and an ear for it. Highlight a variety of authors with a gift for golden prose such as Jane Yolen, Cynthia Rylant, Eve Bunting, or Patricia Polacco.

> ·····► *Tips for talking about it*
>
> A moment of beauty in a text may be made up of multiple sensory details—that is, it goes beyond a visual image. The gem might be a sentence, a phrase, or a passage that not only stirs sight, sound, taste, and smell, but evokes emotional frisson between characters by way of exquisite word choice. Draw attention to how authors create these magical moments. In fiction, this may be a description of a character, setting, or event. In nonfiction, it may be a photograph or descriptive phrase. Highlight these things and discuss both the crafting process and language or visual that accomplishes this.

Emotional: We wouldn't read if the experience didn't engage our emotions. We seem hardwired to seek out stories that help us live in other characters' lives for a while in order to escape or make our own lives understandable. Helping students to articulate *why* they were moved goes a long way to encouraging them to keep finding books that give them the same emotional charge. It is this emotional charge that serves as the flame that ignites more motivated and engaging reading. This is always a key goal of our teaching.

> ·····► *Tips for talking about it*
>
> Encourage students to recognize that everyone has a right to respond to a text as they do. In discussions of emotional moments— or any of the above categories—students are most successful when the teacher sends a strong message that respectful listening and response is the key to enjoying books together. Remind students that these moments are personal to each reader and that we all respond emotionally in different ways since our life experiences, likes, and dislikes are unique. Encourage students to share their own emotional journey and respect the emotional journeys of others who have chosen a different path.

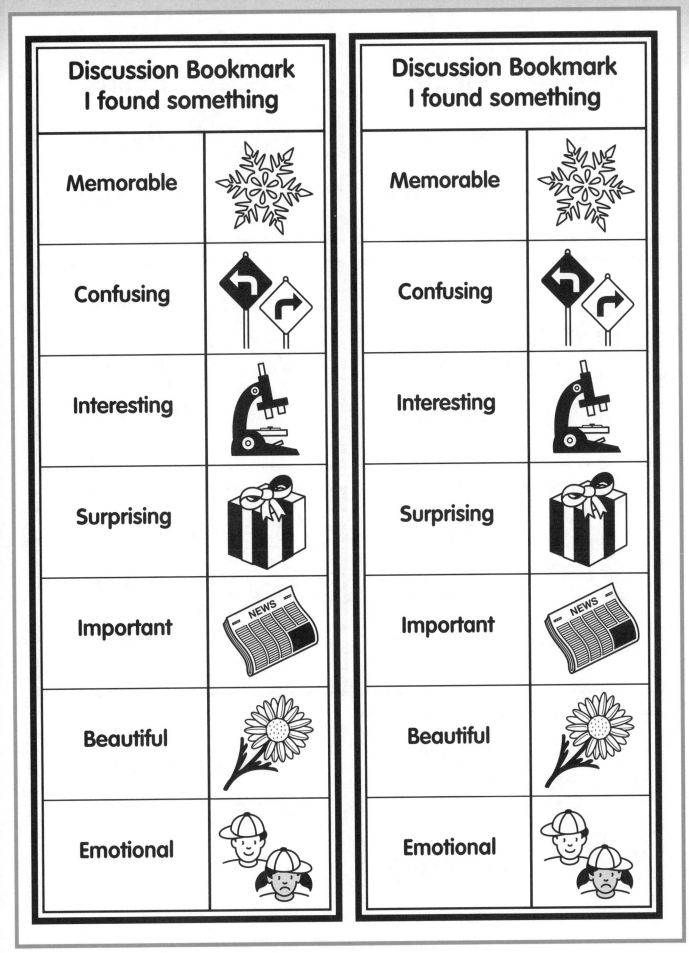

Discussion Bookmark I found something	
Memorable	
Confusing	
Interesting	
Surprising	
Important	
Beautiful	
Emotional	

Discussion Bookmark I found something	
Memorable	
Confusing	
Interesting	
Surprising	
Important	
Beautiful	
Emotional	

I think this is memorable

I think this is important

I think this is confusing

I think this is beautiful

I think this is interesting

I think this is emotional

I think this is surprising

Discussion Prompt Cards

Discussion Prompt Reading Samples

✔	Category	Description of my reading example
	Memorable	
	Confusing	
	Interesting	
	Surprising	
	Important	
	Beautiful	
	Emotional	

Comprehension Gestures

What It Is

Comprehension Gestures are ten hand signs specifically designed to reflect metacognitive processes. These gestures are used during group discussion to increase student awareness of this important category of thinking in the context of reading and to support students in making sense of what they read. The motion is then combined with the students' language to enhance understanding.

Instructional Focus

discussion, writing to support learning

When to Use It

Use these concrete movements during discussion to help support students' understanding of the more abstract concepts associated with comprehension. This will provide multiple sources for understanding and verbalizing this thinking.

What to Do

1. Create a reference tool for the gestures by cutting colored file folders in thirds horizontally. Copy the label and overview strips provided and glue the label to the front and strips to the top and bottom of open folders so the gestures are in the order shown in the figure, Visual Overview of Folder Placement.

2. Introduce two gestures daily in the order they appear on the list using a brief teacher read-aloud to support the comprehension process promoted. Select a text that will provide several opportunities to reinforce that teaching point.

3. After reading, highlight the text sample and describe the comprehension focus as you use the term and gesture simultaneously. Emphasize how the gesture reflects the comprehension process and use the term with the gesture as frequently as possible, referring to an example each time.

4. Encourage students to mirror these movements and to practice gestures as they participate in the discussion of texts. Throughout the discussion, encourage students to add their own ideas as they use the comprehension gesture. Remember to emphasize how each gesture is associated with the thinking.

Teaching Tips

✱ Use your students to create a visual reminder of the gestures. Take a photograph of students posing the gestures and place them on cardstock pages with the comprehension process labeled. Display these around the room for reference. This will make it easier to learn quickly and personalize the thinking gestures. You may even record specific reading examples students suggest to support this thinking.

✱ Create a notebook version of the hand models to explain the comprehension processes. Each open page in the notebook shows the hand model and comprehension process on the right side, with the question associated with each gesture (see Visual Overview of Comprehension Gestures on page 108. You may include specific text examples as appropriate.

✱ Use the form as a literacy center activity revolving around whole-group read-aloud. Each student may be assigned a comprehension process to list on a group form or students may complete these individually or with a partner. The form is then shared in a whole-group setting.

✱ Provide time for students to practice the gestures with a partner using independent reading texts. These self-selected texts will increase motivation and allow students to identify personally relevant examples to practice the gestures and thinking processes.

5. Continue adding two gestures daily, repeating previous movements when possible so that students are continuously associating the thinking with the gestures. This repetition will reinforce the processes and help them to remember the gestures.

6. Once you have taught every gesture, provide many opportunities to put them all together using varied learning experiences. The Comprehension Gestures Planning Form can be used to select a thinking process sample alone or with a partner before sharing. This promotes the thinking strategies while providing many opportunities for students to practice the hand gestures in meaningful contexts.

7. Always keep in mind that the gestures are designed to reinforce and support the thinking processes rather than to undermine them. Some children may drop the gestures once the thinking is in place and this should be respectfully acknowledged and accepted. In some cases, gestures will be used as a temporary scaffold while some children will find them useful for years to come. Strategies should support, not hinder, thinking so let students take the lead.

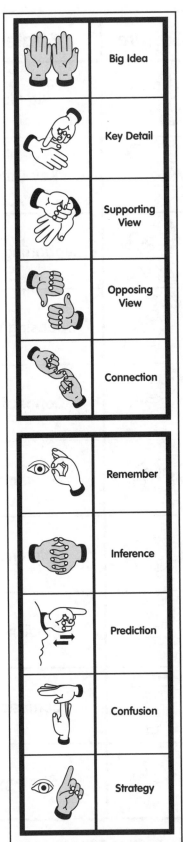

Visual Overview of Folder Placement

Visual Overview of Comprehension Gestures

Gesture	Strategy	Description	Question
	Big Idea	Cup both hands together with the palms up	What is the most important idea you can say in the fewest words?
	Key Detail	Point the index finger into open palm	What are a few of the most important facts or events to emphasize?
	Supporting View	Put fist into open hand and move upward	What ideas do you agree with and how can you support those ideas?
	Opposing View	Thumbs up and thumbs down on opposite hands	What ideas do you disagree with that you can back up or prove?
	Connection	Hook both of the index fingers together	What does this make you think of that is related to it in some way?
	Remember	Place the okay sign at the side of forehead	What are the most important ideas that are worth remembering?
	Inference	Interlock all of the fingers on both hands	What ideas are not stated but are supported by the author's words?
	Prediction	Point to forehead and move finger forward	What ideas do you expect in the next part using the author's clues?
	Confusion	Form a T with two hands in time-out symbol	What ideas are hard to understand and how can you fix that problem?
	Strategy	Flick index finger as if to turn on a lightbulb	What strategy were you able to use that helped you be a smart reader?

Thinking Signs for Memory Folder Labels

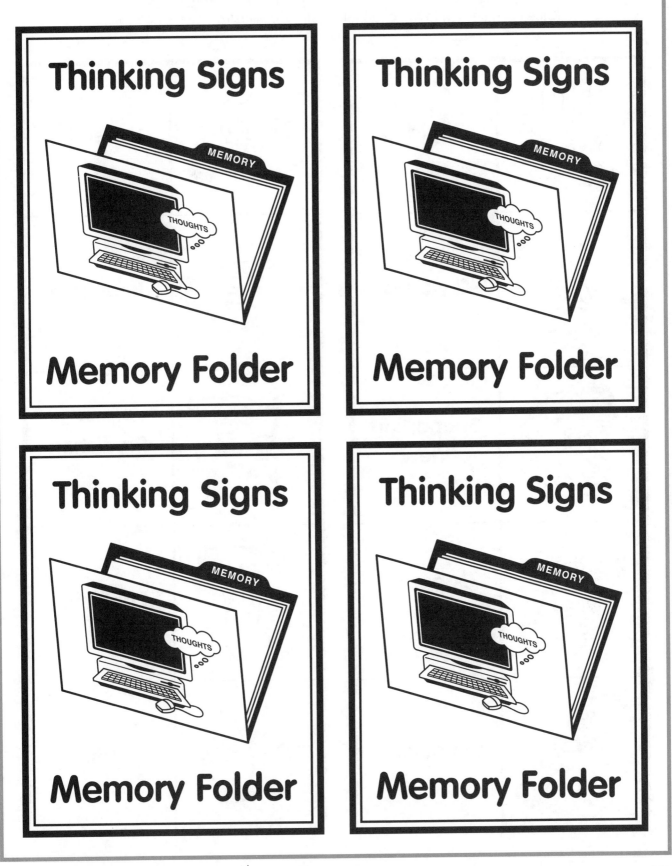

Comprehension Gestures Overview Strips

(Glue each section to the open folder strips as illustrated on page 107.)

	Big Idea		**Remember**
	Key Detail		**Inference**
	Supporting View		**Prediction**
	Opposing View		**Confusion**
	Connection		**Strategy**

Comprehension Gestures Planning Form

Gesture	Strategy	My comprehension example I want to share	Page
	Big Idea		
	Key Detail		
	Supporting View		
	Opposing View		
	Connection		
	Remember		
	Inference		
	Prediction		
	Confusion		
	Strategy		

Reading Strategy Bookmark

What It Is

A Reading Strategy Bookmark is a visual reference of important reading strategies to be used to in the context of meaningful reading. The bookmark is a concrete tool to highlight strategies to transfer to other contexts.

Instructional Focus

reading, writing about reading, discussion

When to Use It

Teachers can use the bookmark to introduce new strategies before reading, to reinforce strategy use during reading, to teach new strategies in the context of reading, and to provide a discussion springboard of good reading strategies after reading.

What to Do

1. Introduce the bookmark as a visual reminder of the important strategies good readers use. Highlight one strategy at a time in a meaningful context, such as shared reading. Place the bookmark next to the book and draw attention to the strategy before, during, and after reading. Bookmarks may be used:

    To set a purpose for reading: "There's a tricky word on this page. See if the pictures help you figure out that hard word."

    To make connections between texts and strategies that have been used in other texts: "Yesterday, we talked about how to look for chunks in words. Read this section and think about whether that strategy is useful here."

    To challenge students to use a specific strategy on their own: "Look for opportunities to use that strategy today as you read your independent book. After reading, I'll ask for examples of how it was useful."

2. The key to building reading proficiency with this tool is to connect the use of the bookmark to discussions that include specific examples from the text. Draw attention to the strategies as they are used directly in reading rather than simply reciting the strategies in isolation. Always make a link between the strategy and reading so the focus is on the application of strategies.

3. Small-group guided reading is the best time to practice using the strategy bookmark since the setting has more individualized and intensive support. This is also an ideal setting in which to use a book at an appropriate level of difficulty so that students will be able to achieve success in using these strategies in a meaningful context. The teacher can also provide a more targeted discussion in these settings.

Teaching Tips

* A smaller mini-bookmark is provided to tape to each student's desk as an ongoing reference. This could remind students of the strategies highlighted in teacher-supported activities as they gain increasing independence.

* Use the form to list specific examples where strategies were helpful. This may be completed with students in an instructional activity or during independent or peer-supported reading. During whole-group reading activities, highlight specific examples as you draw attention to the bookmark. Provide more support in the beginning.

* Strategy strips can be used to highlight a single strategy when the bookmark is being introduced, or strips may be placed directly in a text. You may also duplicate on cardstock several strategy strips that you are emphasizing and tape them together side-by-side. The strategy strips will then stand up in front of the book and surround the student with effective strategies to use during reading. The visual will give him or her a concrete reference of these strategies while the book offers the meaningful context.

* As always, consider these tools as temporary scaffolds that may be dropped as students begin to use strategies on their own. Once students can highlight and discuss strategies and share examples within the context of their reading on their own, these tools will have accomplished the goal intended and may no longer be needed.

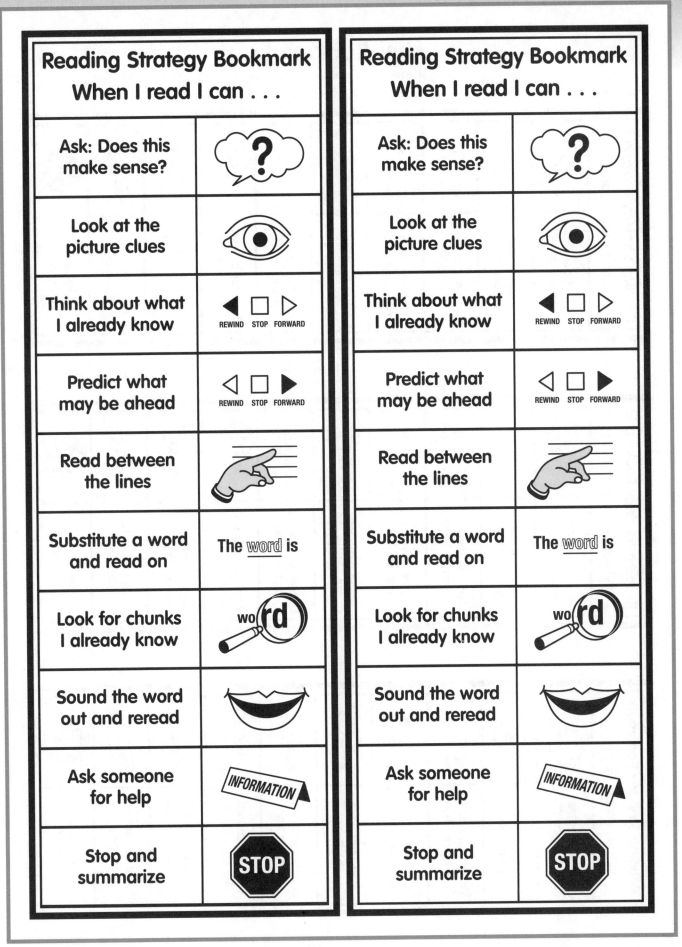

Reading Strategy Bookmark When I read I can . . .	
Ask: Does this make sense?	
Look at the picture clues	
Think about what I already know	REWIND STOP FORWARD
Predict what may be ahead	REWIND STOP FORWARD
Read between the lines	
Substitute a word and read on	The word is
Look for chunks I already know	word
Sound the word out and reread	
Ask someone for help	INFORMATION
Stop and summarize	STOP

Mini-Bookmarks

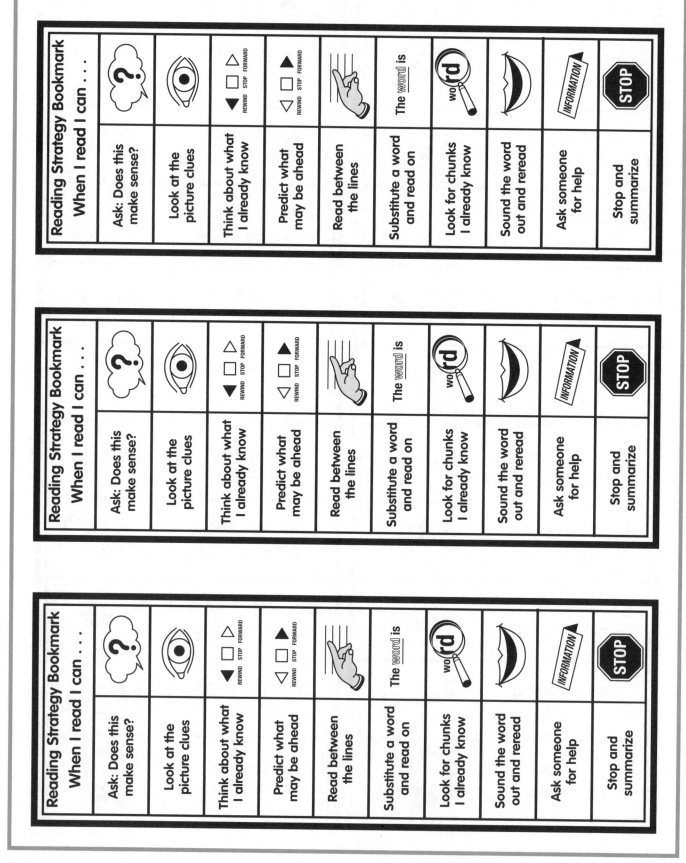

My Reading Strategy Examples

Strategy	Visual	I used this strategy during reading by
Ask: Does this make sense?		
Look at the picture clues		
Think about what I already know	REWIND STOP FORWARD	
Predict what may be ahead	REWIND STOP FORWARD	
Read between the lines		
Substitute a word and read on	The word is	
Look for chunks I already know	word	
Sound the word out and reread		
Ask someone for help	INFORMATION	
Stop and summarize	STOP	

Reading Strategy Strips

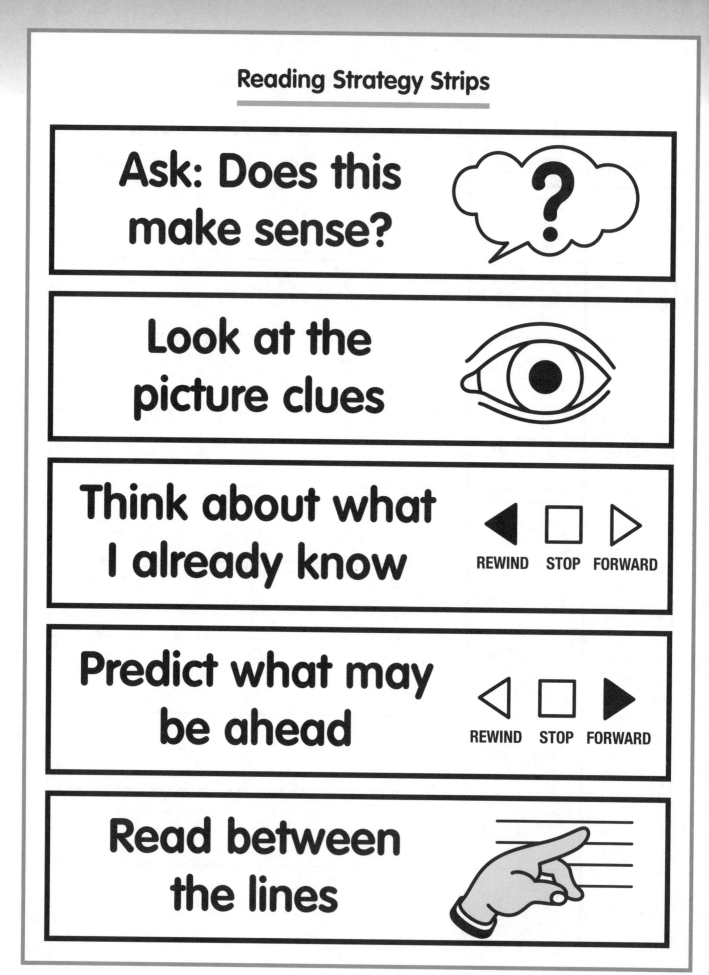

Ask: Does this make sense?

Look at the picture clues

Think about what I already know

REWIND   STOP   FORWARD

Predict what may be ahead

REWIND   STOP   FORWARD

Read between the lines

Reading Strategy Strips

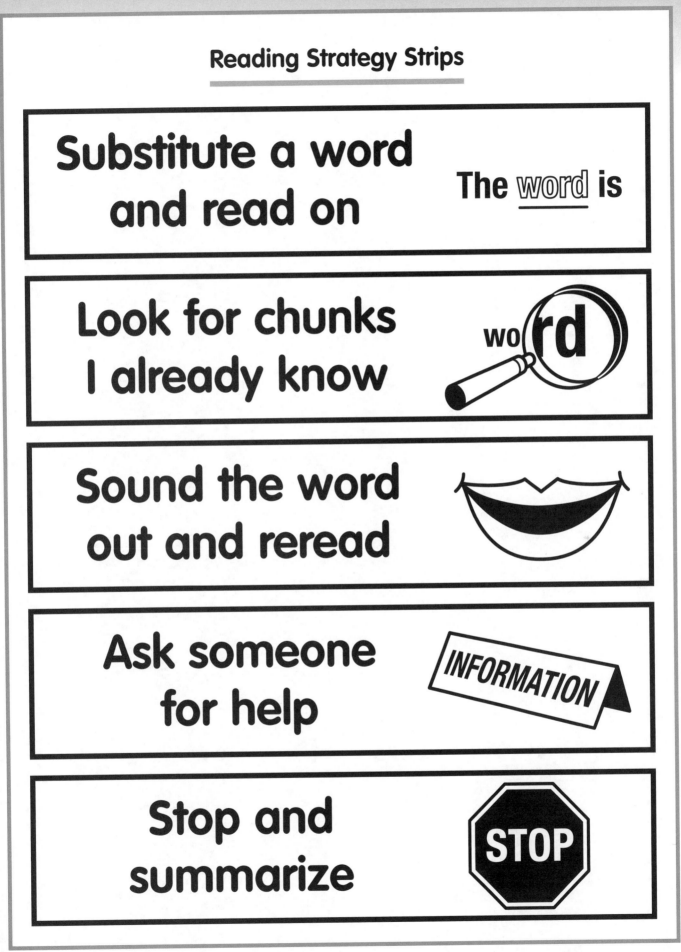

Substitute a word and read on

The <u>word</u> is

Look for chunks I already know

Sound the word out and reread

Ask someone for help

INFORMATION

Stop and summarize

STOP

Reading to Learn

Interactive Note-taking

Memorization is not an accidental event. As adults, we take steps to ensure that we remember important information, from writing ourselves to-do lists each day to highlighting as we read to calling a friend to relate a fascinating radio interview we just heard. Think of the note-taking we did while preparing papers in college or finding a buddy so you could quiz each other in preparation for an exam. And yet in elementary education, teaching memorization techniques has gotten, well, a bad reputation. As if memorizing material is inherently the stuff of "old think" rote learning. Guess what? It's time to help kids secure their understandings. If we cover material and move on, without applying and then revisiting it, we undermine the very purpose of learning. Of course, it must be worth remembering in the first place.

John Medina's *Brain Rules* (2009) offers some interesting facts from neuroscience research to bring to our teaching. First, we must take active steps as we "repeat to remember," to put new learning into our short-term memory within 90 to 120 minutes or much of it is lost. Second, there is a use-it-or-lose-it effect that occurs. In order for us to successfully transfer learning from short-term to long-term memory, we must then "remember to repeat." Yes, repetition and intentional activities that help us commit something to memory are greatly beneficial. In fact, without intent, much new learning will be lost. These frequent opportunities for repetition and review are critical if we want learning to be permanent. I'd even go so far as to say we ought to attend to them at intervals throughout *every* day.

The note-taking activities in this chapter provide specific strategies to achieve this goal as they actively engage students in the learning process and provide a concrete tool to revisit, review, and repeat new learning.

Activities at a Glance

Here is a quick reference to the activities you'll find in this section.

Three-Section Notes

Students learn how to take notes on content area and nonfiction texts using three ways of looking at the same information. These recorded references are then used to review and consolidate learning.

> **Setting:** All settings
>
> **Instructional Focus:** *reading, writing to support learning, discussion*
>
> **Forms:** Three-Section Notes Form

Brain Facts and Brain Words

Students learn how to record and research facts and content-specific words and use this for review, sharing, and discussion.

> **Setting:** All settings
>
> **Instructional Focus:** *reading, writing to support learning, discussion, vocabulary*
>
> **Forms:** Brain Facts, Brain Words

Ear, Eye, and Talk Notes

Students interact with the same information three different ways. The repetitive structure helps long-term recall and provides students with multi-modal ways to learn.

> **Setting:** Whole-group and partner work
>
> **Instructional Focus:** *reading, writing to support learning, discussion*
>
> **Forms:** My Ear, Eye, and Talk Notes

Three-Section Notes

What It Is

Most note-taking methods, such as the Cornell Method, move from detailed notes to key points. While this is a useful approach for more experienced learners, these details can be challenging for struggling readers. Three-Section Notes reverses the sequence by first determining a text's key points and then attending to naming the supporting ideas and summarizing the piece. The three distinct steps give students experience in distinguishing major and minor details, moving from smaller to bigger ideas, and offer an opportunity to consolidate new learning.

Instructional Focus

reading, writing to support learning, discussion

When to Use It

Use this activity to support students when they are reading to learn, specifically when they are reading nonfiction and content area texts.

What to Do

1. Introduce the activity through a teacher read-aloud of a brief informational or nonfiction text or text passage. Teacher demonstration is essential in the early stages, but you'll want to engage students in the process soon as you provide opportunities to apply learning using very brief selections focused on a specific topic. Keep supporting them as needed and gradually increase the length and complexity of the text.

2. After reading the text aloud, think aloud how you decide the key points and write them on the right side of the form. For example, in a passage about polar bears' diminishing habitat, I'd write as key points details such as "ice melts," "land melting away!" "global warming," and "extinction"—and I'd talk through *how* I reasoned that these are the passage's key ideas. Notice that I am including only key words and phrases to explain bigger ideas. I would also think aloud as I add any visuals to support these ideas. Be sure that students understand that you are taking important ideas directly from the text and condensing them for review later.

3. Once you have written the key points to reflect the most important concepts, use these to generate sentences to explain them in more detail (important ideas). This may reflect a single key point or two may be combined. For example, I may combine the key words "extinction" and "land melting away" to cre-

continues

Teaching Tips

* This sequence can be adapted based on the content you read and your instructional goal. You may reverse the order of the steps by recording the supporting details first and then ask students to arrive at the key points, or use a teacher-initiated summary statement *before* reading to support students' comprehension. Students may eventually complete these steps on their own or with a partner, as long as discussion is built into the activity.

* This activity can support students as they learn how to write research reports or nonfiction paragraphs. The completed form can serve almost as an outline to help them generate their composition.

* Use a tape recorder to reinforce these ideas as needed. Students can use the form to record important concepts using the completed form and then listen to the recording as they review the form. This will offer excellent reinforcement for those students who need additional repetition.

Three-Section Notes *(continued)*

ate the sentence, "Polar bears may become extinct as their land melts and disappears." Notice how the key points are used to explain concepts so the wording may change. Draw attention to this thinking

4. Finally, I demonstrate how to craft a brief summary statement, and write it at the bottom of the form. When the form is complete, review important concepts using the entire form. Remind students to look at each section as you discuss the big ideas. Summarization can be a difficult concept for students to learn so spend as much time as needed teaching and reinforcing this thinking.

5. Depending on the grade level you teach, you can get students to participate in this introductory demonstration or have them watch you do it entirely— and then the next day, with another text, you can hand them the reins and have them do most of the thinking. Do not rush through this process, taking the time to build a solid foundation first.

6. Use the form with a wide variety of brief texts in many settings. Each component is important teaching that students will need as proficient readers.

Three-Section Notes

Important ideas

Summary statement

Key points

Brain Facts and Brain Words

What It Is

In Brain Facts and Brain Words students identify and research facts and new vocabulary used in informational texts. Two note-taking forms can be used to incorporate teacher-selected concepts; however, the ultimate goal is to help students identify these key elements independently. Following reading, students select up to five words or facts and record explanations on the form. These concepts are not written verbatim from a text or dictionary, but explained in the student's words using key concepts and a simple sketch to reinforce those concepts visually. The form is then used for sharing purposes.

Instructional Focus

reading, writing to support learning, discussion, vocabulary

When to Use It

This activity can be used in any setting where you're reading and responding to content area and nonfiction texts.

What to Do

1. Begin by modeling through a read-aloud of an informational text. Complete the form together, selecting only one of the forms at a time according to the opportunities afforded by the selection and your learning goals. Copy facts or words that seem important and worth learning more about and take the time to discuss how these are relevant to the topic. For brain words, include the context from the selection.

2. For each fact or word, create a brief explanation and a simple visual explaining your thinking as you complete the form. Engage students in this thinking process and encourage them to contribute their own ideas whenever possible. It is important for them to verbalize thinking orally as you support this process. Highlight learning as needed such as restating new ideas or recording key points.

3. Gradually allow students to assume more control in shared reading activities. An effective approach is to provide peer- or teacher-supported learning to initiate the activity, complete the form independently as you rotate, and then discuss the form with a peer or teacher. Students can also complete two or three words or facts on their own and then collaborate on the rest. How quickly you allow students to assume this added responsibility will depend on the needs of your students. Take as much time as students need at this stage to build a strong foundation for the future.

continues

Teaching Tips

* Use the forms to engage students in a powerful negotiation of learning. Students can work with a partner or small groups to initiate the facts and words. When the form is completed, they can then work with a new partner or group to combine ideas, or even reduce the facts to those that are most relevant to the topic. The dialogue that revolves around this negotiation will offer rich learning opportunities.

* You may create a pool of class words or a brief list of facts for students to select from for a more targeted focus. This extension will give students needed reinforcement since several will have the same word/fact. Form small groups for students to work together to become the "expert" of a specific focus.

* You may also turn these explorations into a wall display or class book with facts and words. This will allow you to highlight key learning points as you create a resource for ongoing review. Students may also do more in-depth research and add new learning points.

4. Some students will need more support in the early learning stages. Use small-group guided reading to offer instructional support or reinforcement as needed, using texts that are at an appropriate level of challenge so that the text demands are not requiring cognitive attention needed for identifying key ideas and words. For some students, it is best to read first and complete the form in a second reading.

5. It is important to provide time for students to share their brain facts/words with others. This will reinforce those concepts and provide an opportunity to discuss the note-taking process. Students can share their learning with peers by rotating to several partners. Emphasize that the goal is to provide an explanation rather than to read from the form, reminding them that varying the explanation will allow them to learn with each new partnership. The form is then used only as a reference tool. Encourage students to add new details they learn during sharing process.

6. End with time for whole-group sharing and review of important points as a class. Discuss these learning points, ask questions, and probe for detail. Don't forget to highlight the use of the note-taking form so that you emphasize the relevance of this study and learning strategy and how it can be used with greater independence in the future. You may use this time to create a class summary of key ideas revolving around the topic for display.

7. Some students will find the simple design of forms helpful. Make these, and other forms in this book, available for those students to use on their own as appropriate. Let students be your guide

Brain Facts

Name _____

Topic _____

Quick Sketch	The most important points I need to remember

Summary Review

1. _____

2. _____

3. _____

4. _____

5. _____

Habitat
Camouflage
Hibernation

Brain Words

Word	Quick Sketch	My Personal Explanation
1		
2		
3		
4		
5		

Ear, Eye, and Talk Notes

What It Is

Ear, Eye, and Talk Notes is a note-taking strategy that allows students to learn the same information in three different ways through listening (ear), reading (eye), and discussing (talk). The repetitive structure helps long-term recall and provides excellent assessment information. It also provides a discussion forum about how students learn new information most effectively and in what sequence.

Instructional Focus

reading, writing to support learning, discussion

When to Use It

Use this activity with brief informational selections that contain a complete idea. The note-taking form provides a resource for discussion and review of the material.

What to Do

1. Select a brief informational selection with a clearly stated main idea. Review the concepts and create an oral preview of the informational selection with some key details omitted that your students can identify later. You may record these concepts in the form of notes, but this will be used only as an overview for planning.

2. Students listen as you provide your oral preview. It is important that you explain these ideas in an engaging way rather than simply reading them from your notes. Students do not have the text in front of them, so as they watch you they gain important information not only through your words but your facial expressions, gestures, and other nonverbal communication. This will set the stage for the learning that occurs after listening.

3. Model the Ear Notes as a think-aloud in the beginning, although eventually students will do this on their own. Demonstrate that notes are recorded in bulleted points using key words and phrases with visuals when needed. Think aloud as you add these ideas. This will be important support you can relinquish later.

4. When the Ear Notes are completed, provide students with the text and read it to or with them in the beginning. Complete the Eye Notes collaboratively with students to model this process. These are notes students take based on the full informational selection. Students will add any missing details to their notes that were not included in Ear Notes. Students can also correct any errors under Ear Notes such as inaccurate information or misspellings acknowledged during reading that were not available during the listening phase.

continues

Teaching Tips

* The sequence of note-taking offers insight into the learning approach that is most effective for students. The discussion that accompanies this learning activity will be equally important to understanding how students learn and making them privy to this knowledge.

* Ear, Eye, Talk integrates essential approaches for note-taking, including collaboration, variety, dialogue, and repetition. This will require additional time, so use only brief texts and targeted concepts of learning so that you do not compromise these added demands by sacrificing any of the critical steps.

* Incorporate these sequences into your daily teaching and encourage students to use these preferences in their own learning activities. Every learning activity is an opportunity for you to understand the needs of your students as well as for students to understand and appreciate their own learning differences and strengths.

Ear, Eye, and Talk Notes *(continued)*

5. Now have students work on their Talk Notes. Instruct students to work in pairs to discuss the text and take notes on their discussion. Using the form and text as a reference, students will discuss what they learned and add any new points at the bottom of the form as they learn from peers. Rotate to monitor and support students' understanding of the task. Students may also work with more than one partner, adding new learning as they move around the room sharing ideas. They will enjoy watching their learning grow and sharing ideas with others. In some cases, it may be a visual used to reinforce a concept as students learn how others visually represent their thinking.

6. At the completion of the activity, discuss the three ways of approaching the material. Which worked best for which students? Ask students to consider how processing the information all three ways helped them learn it better. Some students will recall few things in Ear Notes while they will add many details in Eye Notes, suggesting that listening is more challenging. Other students may record many details in Ear Notes while adding few details in Eye Notes, suggesting either a text that is too challenging or that more concentrated attention is needed during reading. Emphasize that each learner has different strengths that warrant different approaches, and suggest how they can use these strengths in other learning activities.

7. Reverse the order on another occasion so that, for example, students take Eye Notes before Ear Notes or consider adding Talk Notes after each sequence (which is extremely effective for some students). Be flexible, always remembering that differentiation is about adjusting the learning activity to meet the needs of every student and helping them to understand how they learn. Take advantage of the rich assessment information afforded you by making anecdotal notes as you rotate.

My Ear Notes

My Eye Notes

My Talk Notes

Maintaining Effective Instruction

Assessment Forms

Ongoing assessment is integral to the RTI model, or any effective literacy design. With the understanding that good instruction ensures that each student experiences success, we should use assessment to help us to increase the quality of our instruction and determine how well we have accomplished this. Varied assessments are needed to accomplish this goal, including formal and informal assessments that range in time, context, setting, and purpose. Without these varied markers, we run the risk of misinterpreting data since we lose so much information when we focus on narrow concepts of learning.

While numerical values are commonly associated with assessment in the RTI model, this is not the only way to measure students' growth as readers, writers, and thinkers. The assessment forms in this section are designed to inform the instructional process so that each activity is implemented in the most effective way. Much of your assessment is rooted in instruction when you observe your students as they actively engage in a learning activity so that assessment and instruction are woven together. This day-to-day formative assessment is "at the heart of the daily decision-making process within an RTI classroom" (Owocki 2010, 9). The more assessment is isolated from instruction, the more we stand to lose.

While using the activities in this book, you've observed how the instruction is presented in such a way that you have multiple opportunities to assess students before, during, and after learning. As you implement the activities to gently nudge students to new understanding or reinforce learning, ask probing questions and listen for information about the student's thinking. Purposeful dialogue will support you in fine-tuning or adjusting teaching.

A question frequently posed is whether the activities can be used for grading purposes. Yes, you can assign a grade to any activity as long as you target a specific focus. But one needs to reverse the traditional perspective; instead, the purpose of instruction is to design a learning experience that *may* lead to a grade *if* the value of the learning activity takes priority. Grades are one more marker that can help improve student learning if we ask ourselves some important questions: Is it a true reflection of success? How can you create a more successful learning experience in the future? A thoughtful and reflective teacher is needed to make these adjustments.

An important goal of the RTI model is to identify students who are not making adequate progress so that we can offer support before the gap widens. To be responsive, ongoing monitoring is needed so that we can quickly identify students in need of more intensive learning opportunities in or beyond the classroom setting. The forms in this chapter are designed as a monitoring system rather than a process of collecting numerical data. As you use these activities, several guidelines will help you assume a more responsive assessment stance.

Learn to *stop, look,* and *listen* as you reflect more closely on each stage of learning. If students experience success, consider what you can replicate in this or other contexts for continued success. If students do not experience success, pinpoint the problem—and then make adjustments to your teaching that will guarantee success in the future. Identify which students need more support from you; which students can move forward with peer support; and which students need your undivided, one-on-one attention to guide them toward independence.

Look beyond what the student writes and consider what it reflects about each student. Is the thinking logical? Is a sequential step in the process missing? Does a student struggle to formulate an idea or is it more about getting those ideas in printed form? Does the students' work tell me that more discussion is needed at a particular stage of learning? Consider how each completed form can inform your teaching and support the adjustments that will enhance learning. Maintain a proactive stance as you acknowledge your critical role in this process.

Honestly reflect on your role in creating a successful learning experience. Did you explicitly model the activity to ensure understanding before relinquishing control to students? Did you explain the task and learning expectations? Did you withdraw the guided practice support too soon? Are there any gaps in knowledge that would prohibit a successful experience? How can you fill those gaps? Look beyond the accuracy of responses to consider what they tell you and how *you* can change your actions to ensure learning in the future. Your active role will ultimately determine the success or failure of each student, so carefully reflect on these changes.

Look for individual strengths that will lead to greater success in the future. Does the student excel during oral responses, but struggle to put those ideas in writing? How can oral language expression support written expression? Is peer-supported collaboration needed as students gain independence? How can you increase success by making any adjustments that acknowledge the unique capabilities every student brings to the literacy table? Even in a sea of faces, we can individualize when we become more thoughtful observers and make the necessary adjustments to meet the needs of each child. This can't be scripted. It requires the moment by moment decision making that is the hallmark of effective teaching.

Differentiate in or beyond the context of the initial learning activity. Develop a sharper assessment lens to offer additional support to highlight student needs in more intensive settings. Be flexible as you adjust the focus, sequence, or resources in teacher-supported activities according to student need. Form a small group to set the stage *before* a class activity, target specific needs *during* the activity as others work on their own or with peers, or form a small group *after* the activity using appropriate alternative methods or resources. What targeted support can you offer to ensure success?

Initiate individual conferences revolving around the learning activity to better understand each student. Encourage students to verbalize their own thinking so that dialogue can turn into responsive instruction. These experiences will lead to more successful learning experiences in the future because they will inform instruction as they inform students' ability to assume greater control of their own learning successes. Always remember that each learning activity is an opportunity to enrich the learning experiences that follow. This springboard to future success is the ultimate "pot at the end of the rainbow."

Generate supportive dialogue rather than criticism.
Red marks on a student's paper only reflect what we fail to teach and do nothing to support the child in increasing success in later efforts. Our goal is not to point out what students did wrong, but instead to use discussion to gently nudge students toward the thinking that leads to success. Look at each new learning experience from the student's perspective and offer any support necessary to turn these challenges into successes. Ultimately, their successes and failures are a direct reflection of our successes and failures as well. Good teachers acknowledge this responsibly.

Use these activities in other areas of instruction during the day and apply what you learn to new learning experiences. Consider the successes as well as the challenges students face and let this inform how you design other activities. None of these activities are meant to stand alone. The open-ended nature of each of the forms in this book allows you to provide a wide range of learning experiences across the curriculum. Each learning experience has the power to inform your teaching and the quality of your instruction. Use what you learn about students as they are actively engaged in learning throughout the day.

Include many forms of feedback, including teacher assessment, self-assessment, and peer collaboration.
Assessment embedded within a learning activity allows each instructional activity to enrich those that follow. Use these opportunities to establish learning goals and initiate the support students need. Assessment should reflect learning in that it includes time to revisit, rethink, revise, and modify ideas. Multiple forms of feedback give students the specific tools they will need as we enrich the learning process and dramatically increase the potential of future successes.

Monitor learning with a concrete system that helps you look for patterns. Use Stoplight Assessment Folders to organize activities according to student need. Use a red folder for students who will need small-group support with daily or weekly monitoring, a yellow folder for students who will need less intensive support with weekly or biweekly monitoring, and a green folder for those students who are currently achieving success and are monitored only biweekly or monthly. This organizational strategy can help you plan and implement new learning experiences according to need. Create a new set of Stoplight folders for each learning activity, since placement in the folders may change with the text, instructional focus, or the complexity of a task.

A variety of assessment forms are provided in this chapter to support you as you implement the activities in this book. Select only those that are appropriate, modifying and adding what you need. Never forget that learning begins with you, so your involvement is essential. Assessment, and the instruction this assessment informs, is not what we do *to* our students, but what we do *for* them so that we can increase their success today and tomorrow. You play the most important role in any effective instructional or assessment design. This does not come from viewing a flashy spreadsheet, but from watching and interacting with students engaged in the learning process and gleaning how that knowledge can enhance your teaching.

Once again, the *you* factor rings true because *you* matter, my friends.

Strategy Implementation Record

Teacher _____ Grade _____

Date	Page	Strategy Name	Personal Adaptations	✔

Instructional Planning Checklist

General Strategy Questions

Key questions to ask at each stage of learning	My Reflections/Goals
Questions to ask *before* the activity: ☐ What will I do to set the stage for the learning activity? ☐ What student knowledge is needed to ensure success? ☐ How will I fill any existing gaps in knowledge? ☐ Do students know how to use the resources needed? ☐ How will I adequately model the thinking process? ☐ Do students need to use a specific sequence of steps? ☐ How much teacher support will be needed at this time?	
Questions to ask *during* the activity: ☐ Do students demonstrate that they understand the task? ☐ Are students using appropriate sequential progression? ☐ Can students record ideas logically in written form? ☐ What do I notice when I rotate as students work? ☐ What supports do I offer to ensure student success? ☐ What adjustments do I make to differentiate learning? ☐ Do I encourage peer collaboration throughout learning?	
Questions to ask *after* the activity: ☐ Do I look beyond accuracy to understand thinking? ☐ Do I probe to gather more information for teaching? ☐ Can students use available resources to justify ideas? ☐ Can students summarize learning in their own words? ☐ What small-group extension activities will be needed? ☐ What other contexts will help transfer understanding? ☐ What new instruction will enhance understanding?	

Strategy Analysis and Planning Form

Strategy _____

Key questions to ask at each stage of learning	Goals and Objectives
What specific actions led to increased success?	
What specific challenges did students face?	
What adjustments can I make in the future?	
What is my next step? ☐ Repeat the strategy using a new text/context/setting ☐ Repeat the strategy with selected adjustments ☐ Offer more intensive support in small-group settings ☐ Use a related strategy (_____) ☐ Teach a new strategy (_____)	

Needs-Assessment Instructional Questions

Strategy _____

Key questions to ask at each stage of learning	Student Support Needs
Before learning questions: Does the child . . .	
☐ understand each step of the activity task?	
☐ have adequate prior knowledge and experience?	
☐ possess specific strengths that can be emphasized?	
☐ actively participate in the demonstration model?	
☐ need additional teacher-supported models?	
☐ activate personal experiences to support learning?	
☐ appear motivated to meet the learning demands?	
During learning questions: Does the child . . .	
☐ use appropriate resources to support the task?	
☐ complete the activity without relying on support?	
☐ use the text to support oral and written responses?	
☐ put ideas in printed form to get a message across?	
☐ combine written and visual learning references?	
☐ interact meaningfully during peer collaboration?	
☐ assume increasing responsibility for learning?	
After learning questions: Does the child . . .	
☐ use written references that will support sharing?	
☐ refer to the text to find samples to support ideas?	
☐ verbalize thinking to justify personal understanding?	
☐ summarize key learning points orally or in writing?	
☐ combine new learning with existing knowledge?	
☐ assume increasing control as support is withdrawn?	
☐ respond meaningfully to teacher or peer questions?	

Daily Learning Ritual Activity Evaluation Form

Assessment Focus	Activity Planning Goals
### Activity Selections ☐ Are the activity task selections meaningful? ☐ Is the focus on reading and writing tasks? ☐ Do activities promote active engagement? ☐ Are tasks at appropriate levels of challenge? ☐ Do activities accommodate unique needs? ☐ Are variety and student choice offered?	
### Management Rituals ☐ Are new procedures modeled as added? ☐ Are clear activity guidelines provided? ☐ Is debriefing used to ensure understanding? ☐ Are students actively engaged in learning? ☐ Is increasing independence promoted? ☐ Are adjustments made as needed?	
### Daily Assessment ☐ Do I reflect on student success regularly? ☐ Do I confer with students as needed? ☐ Do I engage students in self-assessment? ☐ Do I include peer-supported assessment? ☐ Do I offer individual support as needed? ☐ Do I adjust activities to grow with students?	

Daily Choice Folder Planning Record

Teacher _____ Grade _____

No.	Activity Option Description	Student Observations
1		
2		
3		
4		
5		
B O N U S		

Weekly Independent Reading Option Planning Record

Activity	Activity that will build student's independence	Activity that will build student's independence	Activity
Independent Reading			Book Bag Reading
Poetry Basket			Fluency Folder
Guest Reader			Traveling Reader
Buddy Reading			Read to the Teacher
Recording Center			Listening Center
Golden Book Response			Golden Book Reading

Instructional Planning Questions

Learning Reflection Journal

Key questions to ask at each stage of learning	Setting Goals
Selecting the Learning Objectives ☐ What key instructional objectives will I highlight? ☐ What sequence will I use to introduce objectives? ☐ What text will provide the framework for each objective? ☐ What are the learning points I want to emphasize? ☐ What key ideas do I want students to record? ☐ Are there any visuals I can use to support learning? ☐ How will I check for understanding after learning?	
Teaching the Learning Objectives ☐ Do I begin with a meaningful context (text-based)? ☐ Do I record key points as a written reference? ☐ Do I engage students in learning with support? ☐ Do I encourage students to justify their own thinking? ☐ Can students transfer key points to the learning journal? ☐ Do students personalize learning with visual references? ☐ Do I summarize important learning concepts?	
Applying the Learning Objectives ☐ Are students actively engaged as they apply learning? ☐ Is there time for students to share and discuss learning? ☐ Do I provide varied contexts to apply learning? ☐ Do I encourage peer collaboration and dialogue? ☐ Are students assuming increasing independence? ☐ Do I revisit the student application page regularly? ☐ What supports should I offer based on observations?	

Learning Reflection Journal Planning Form

Teacher _____ Grade _____

No.	Objective	Key Teaching Points	Student Application

Student Anchor Chart Planning Form

Lesson Focus _____

Key Instructional Concepts	Student Observations

Research Anchor Chart Planning Form

Topic _____

Teacher Research Questions	Student Observations
Key Vocabulary	

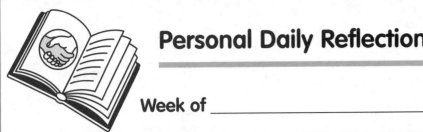

Personal Daily Reflection Record

Week of _____

Instructional Focus	Student Support Needs
Supporting Daily Reflection ☐ Do I regularly summarize new learning concepts? ☐ Do I draw attention to important learning points? ☐ Do I help students brainstorm learning ideas? ☐ Do I encourage students to explain these ideas? ☐ Do I demonstrate how to record learning points? ☐ Do I offer support as students record their ideas? ☐ Do I acknowledge personal ideas as legitimate?	
Selecting Learning Points ☐ Can students identify specific learning concepts? ☐ Can students orally explain learning before writing? ☐ Can students put their ideas in written form? ☐ Can students restate their ideas verbally? ☐ Do I celebrate relevant learning for students? ☐ Do I ask questions to encourage more detail? ☐ Do I provide individual support as needed?	
Peer and Teacher Sharing ☐ Do students share with several partners daily? ☐ Do students use the form as a sharing reference? ☐ Can students respond to questions about learning? ☐ Do students ask relevant questions of their partner? ☐ Do students elaborate beyond the form in sharing? ☐ Do I confer with all students on a weekly basis? ☐ How can I use this information to inform teaching?	

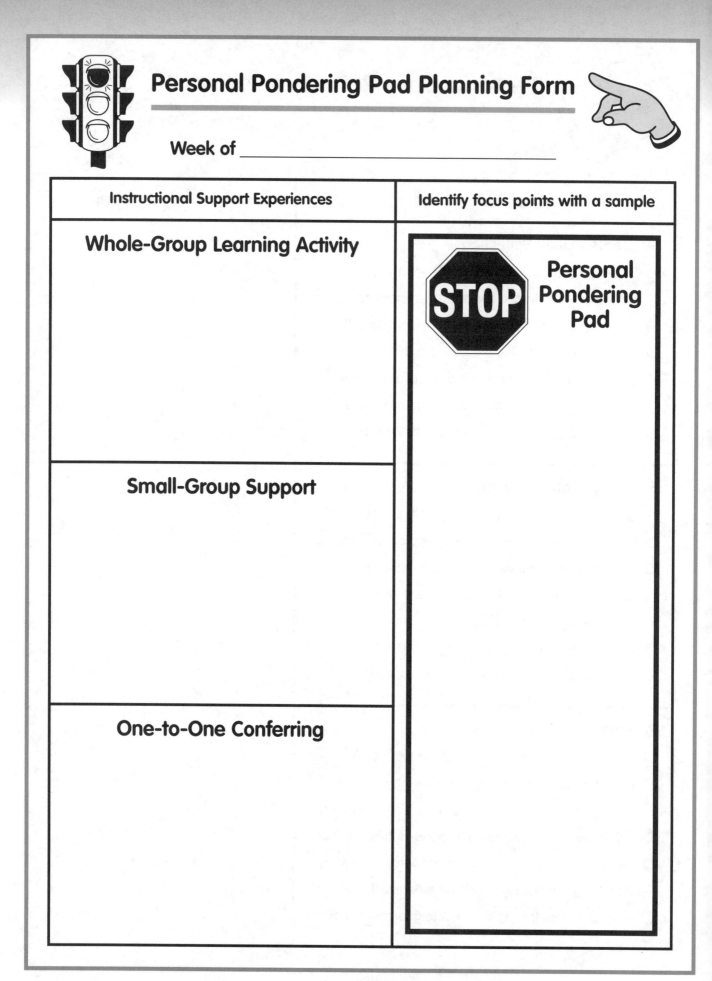

Personal Pondering Pad Planning Form

Week of _____

Instructional Support Experiences	Identify focus points with a sample
Whole-Group Learning Activity	**STOP** Personal Pondering Pad
Small-Group Support	
One-to-One Conferring	

Focus Card Instructional Planning Form

Instructional Focus	Student Support Needs
Focus point recorded on student form	
Key learning concepts to be emphasized	

Instructional Questions

☐ Can students restate and explain the focus point?

☐ Do students use the focus point during reading?

☐ Do students stop at key points to focus attention?

☐ Can students maintain focus throughout reading?

☐ Can students find key ideas to support the focus?

☐ Do students use the text to record discussion points?

☐ Do students use the form to support peer sharing?

☐ Can students evaluate their ability to focus attention?

Summary Preview Instructional Planning Form

Topic _____ Date _____

Instructional focus during each stage of reading	Details I want to highlight
Questions to ask *before* reading (using the preview) ☐ What are the key points I want to preview? ☐ What concepts will set a purpose before reading? ☐ Did I preview ideas without giving too much detail? ☐ Is the preview written at an easier readability level? ☐ How much support will I offer during the preview? ☐ How will I orally state the purpose for reading?	
Questions to ask *during* reading (finding new details) ☐ Do students recognize repeated ideas in the preview? ☐ Can students underline related points in the preview? ☐ Do students identify new details to support the preview? ☐ Can students record ideas using key words or visuals? ☐ Do students use the text to support these new details? ☐ Can students orally explain learning points recorded?	
Questions to ask *after* reading (sharing new learning) ☐ Do students use the form to review learning concepts? ☐ Do students connect the preview to text information? ☐ Can students identify important learning concepts? ☐ Do students add new ideas learned in peer sharing? ☐ Can students provide a general summary of learning? ☐ Can students review learning using the new detail strips?	

Dictionary Redefinition Review Form

Word _____ **Date** _____

Instructional Focus	Support Needs
Dictionary Definition *(Can students . . .)* ☐ use dictionary references to locate words? ☐ select a definition to fit the context offered? ☐ identify words in definitions that are familiar? ☐ select helpful words to use for the redefinition? ☐ identify words in definitions that are confusing? ☐ consider alternate words to clarify learning points?	
Student Redefinition *(Can students . . .)* ☐ look for additional context clues in the text? ☐ use key points in the definition to support learning? ☐ add appropriate details to the initial definition? ☐ incorporate new learning in the definition? ☐ create a new definition that includes these details? ☐ include text samples to support the meaning?	
Peer Collaboration *(Can students . . .)* ☐ summarize new learning to reflect word knowledge? ☐ add a visual reference to support word learning? ☐ incorporate text information to explain the word? ☐ combine the definition and redefinition for sharing? ☐ add additional learning as a result of peer sharing? ☐ use the form as a word study learning reference?	

Reader's Toolbox Instructional Points

Week of _____

✔	Categories	Important Concepts to Highlight	Support Needs
	character		
	quote		
	setting		
	vocabulary		
	BIG idea		
	key details		
	WOW!		
	question		

Instructional Planning Checklist

Word Study and Review Activities

Key questions to ask at each stage of learning	Support Goals
Selecting Words ☐ Do students select words that will challenge them? ☐ Do those words reflect students' current needs? ☐ Are some words repeated for ongoing reinforcement? ☐ Are words personally relevant to students' interests? ☐ Do students put careful thought into word selection? ☐ Do students use words with meaningful contexts? ☐ Do words reflect reading, writing, and meaning goals?	
Learning Words ☐ Do students use varied modalities to learn words? ☐ Do students use written supports to practice words? ☐ Do learning activities access varied memory pathways? ☐ Do students initiate daily practice of selected words? ☐ Can students generate personal definitions of words? ☐ Can students create a visual representation of words? ☐ Can students create and use word learning references?	
Teaching Words ☐ Do students actively engage the listener in learning? ☐ Do students move beyond definitions with explanations? ☐ Can students describe personal learning strategies? ☐ Do students share varied aspects of word knowledge? ☐ Do students include relationships between words? ☐ Can students summarize important learning points? ☐ Do students support the listener in learning words?	

Ongoing Record of Word Learning

Word Learning Strategy _____

Date	Student/s	Word/s	✓

Open-Ended Self-Assessment Word Graph

Student _____ **Dates** _____

Learning Focus _____

List word selections below
(color-code words on chart)

| 1 | 2 | 3 | 4 | 5 | 6 | 7 | 8 | 9 | 10 |

→
Date

Before Learning Goals:

I am proud of these accomplishments:

Using a Class Pool of Words to Achieve Expert Status

Title/Topic _____ Date _____

No.	Target Word	Student Expert Groups	Key Learning Points
1			
2			
3			
4			
5			

Climbing the Word Expert Ladder

How much do students know about the selected words?

- ☐ brief summary
- ☐ real-life example
- ☐ book example
- ☐ personal definition
- ☐ part of speech
- ☐ pronunciation
- ☐ illustration
- ☐ spelling pattern
- ☐ multiple meaning
- ☐ synonym
- ☐ antonym
- ☐ root word
- ☐ dictionary definition

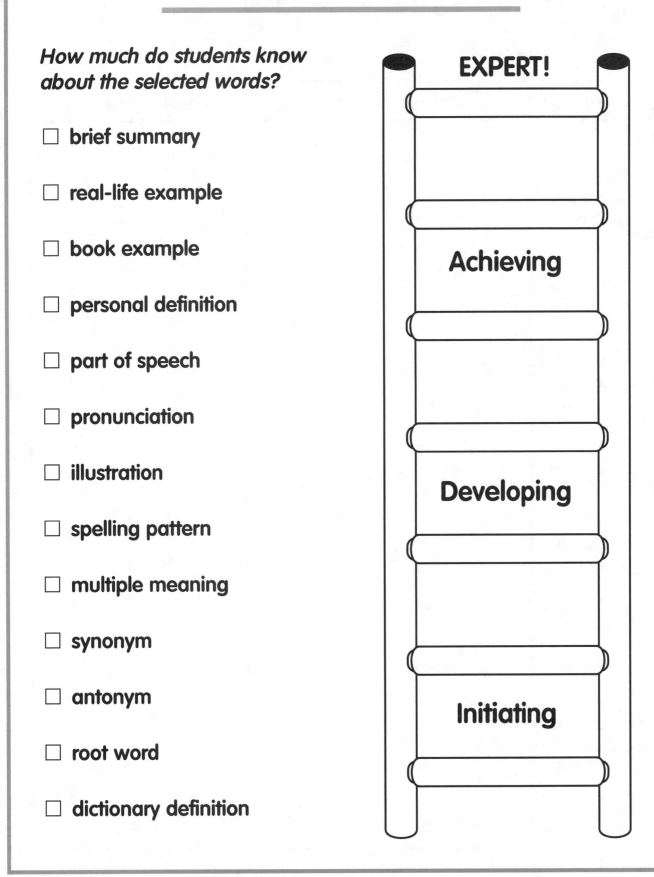

EXPERT!

Achieving

Developing

Initiating

Adopt-a-Word Learning Record

Week of _____

Students can	Overview of observations	Student support needs
Select a relevant word to learn		
Use the word in meaningful contexts		
Recognize the word in printed form		
Demonstrate new learning over time		

"Living" Vocabulary Instructional Review

Word _____ Date _____

Instructional Focus	Support Needs
Initiating word meaning: (Can students . . .)	
☐ verbalize an initial meaning using the text context?	
☐ explore the word using appropriate references?	
☐ select and record a definition based on the context?	
☐ use word knowledge to create a personal definition?	
☐ identify related words that fit the context?	
☐ create a visual representation to support meaning?	
☐ discuss and plan for the posed representation?	
☐ engage in creating an appropriate photograph?	
☐ explain the word meaning orally using new learning?	
☐ demonstrate a deeper understanding of the word?	
Practicing and learning words: (Can students . . .)	
☐ use the form to discuss growing word knowledge?	
☐ create a reference card to revisit key concepts?	
☐ use the card and all resources to practice the word?	
☐ discuss the word with peers using new learning?	
☐ elaborate on words by explaining over defining?	
☐ add new learning from other word learning activities?	
☐ practice words independently or with peers?	
☐ draw connections between new and previous words?	
☐ demonstrate continued word knowledge over time?	
☐ use word learning to support new word study?	

Classroom CODE RED Word Learning Record

STOP

Teacher _____ **Grade** _____

Entry Date	Code Red Word	Small-Group Word Work Activities	Exit Date

Stoplight Vocabulary Selection Record

Title _____ Week of _____

Categories	Instructional Learning Points	Word Pool
STOP		
YIELD		
GO		

Five-by-Five Partner Reading Reflection Form

Week of _____

Instructional Focus	Student Support Needs
Text Selection ☐ Is the text easy enough to promote independence? ☐ Are there a few challenges for repeated practice? ☐ Is there an appropriate portion of text to practice? ☐ Is the child motivated to read multiple times? ☐ Is time provided to select and practice the reading?	
Repeated Reading ☐ Can the child self-evaluate the first reading? ☐ Are new goals selected for subsequent readings? ☐ Does the child read with increasing expression? ☐ Do the repeated readings improve over time? ☐ Can the child identify specific improvements?	
Word Selection ☐ Are the words relevant for personal learning? ☐ Is the child motivated to learn the words? ☐ Do the words support your instructional goals? ☐ Is the teacher engaged in word selection? ☐ Is motivation and self-selection considered?	
Word Learning ☐ Does the child participate in daily word practice? ☐ Is daily collaboration encouraged to learn words? ☐ Can the child identify related words for extension? ☐ Does the child notice relationships between words? ☐ Is learning demonstrated at the end of the week?	

Five-by-Five Partner Reading Observation Form

Week of _____

Student	Text Selection	Meaning/Fluency	Word Learning

Read, Listen, and Think

Weekly Student Reflection

Review Date	Student Name	Effective Strategy Use	Instructional Points	Share ✓

G O A L S	

Classroom Sharing Bookmark Record

Title Selection _____

	Specific Text Samples to Highlight	Page
My Sharing Bookmark I think this is: ☐ Important ☐ Challenging ☐ Memorable Name _____	Important	
	Challenging	
	Memorable	

Classroom Jigsaw Vocabulary Assessment

Teacher _____ Grade _____

Assessment Focus	Achieving	In Progress	Support
Assuming Expert Status • engages in peer collaboration • uses a variety of references • explores word relationships • moves beyond a surface meaning • creates a personalized meaning			
Student as Teacher • explains words beyond a definition • offers specific and varied examples • responds to partner questions • offers support for peer learner • checks for understanding			
Student as Learner • restates the word meaning • asks meaningful questions • summarizes word knowledge • integrates personal understanding • records key concepts on the form			

Comments and Goal Setting

Classroom Jigsaw Vocabulary Planning Form

Teacher _____ **Date** _____

Note: Select a limited number of word study options each week

✓	Word Study Options	Jigsaw Groups	Observations
	dictionary definition	**Jigsaw 1**	
	personal definition		
	context clues		
	real-life example	**Jigsaw 2**	
	student illustration		
	part of speech		
	pronunciation key	**Jigsaw 3**	
	synonym		
	antonym		
	root word	**Jigsaw 4**	
	spelling patterns		
	multiple meaning		
	comparing meaning	**Jigsaw 5**	
	syllables		
	related spelling (homonym/homograph)		

Classroom Jigsaw Vocabulary Selection Record

Teacher _____ Grade _____

Date	Selection Source	Word 1	Word 2	Word 3	Word 4	Word 5

Classroom Jigsaw Text Assessment

Teacher _____ **Grade** _____

Assessment Focus	Achieving	In Progress	Support
Establishing a Meaning Base • collaborates in the initial reading • participates in peer discussion • helps to select important points • negotiates the final selection • identifies a personal selection			
Creating Recorded Notes • identifies appropriate key points • reduces ideas to key words/phrases • uses bulleted points to organize • identifies visuals to support ideas • uses notes to review information			
Teaching Key Learning Points • uses key points to explain in detail • uses the visual to build meaning • responds appropriately to questions • offers additional details as needed • helps the learner translate notes			
Comments and Goal Setting			

Classroom Jigsaw Text Record

Topic _____ Grade _____

No.	Jigsaw Members	Learning Focus	Observations
J I G S A W 1			
J I G S A W 2			
J I G S A W 3			
Instructional Goals			

Jigsaw Poetry Reading Assessment Form

Teacher _____ **Grade** _____

Assessment Focus	Achieving	In Progress	Support
Establishing a Meaning Base • participates in meaningful discussion • uses the print to support discussion • summarizes important concepts • offers details to highlight meaning • retells key points in sequential order			
Creating an Expressive Rendition • uses appropriate phrasing • explores varied interpretations • adjusts pacing and vocal inflections • reads with enthusiasm • demonstrates expert reader status			
Exploring an Instructional Focus • explains key points of learning • selects appropriate text samples • identifies examples beyond the text • collaborates to share ideas • uses appropriate resources			
Comments and Goal Setting			

Jigsaw Poetry Reading Planning Form

Title _____ Week of _____

Description of Activities	Jigsaw Groups	Observations
Shared Reading (Introduction)		
Skill Focus (Small-Group Study)		
Repeated Practice (Sharing)		
"Hollywood" Day (Fluency)		

Jigsaw Poetry Reading Selection Record

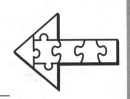

Teacher _____ Grade _____

Date	Title of Poem	Teaching Focus	Comments

Teacher Discussion Prompt Questioning Record

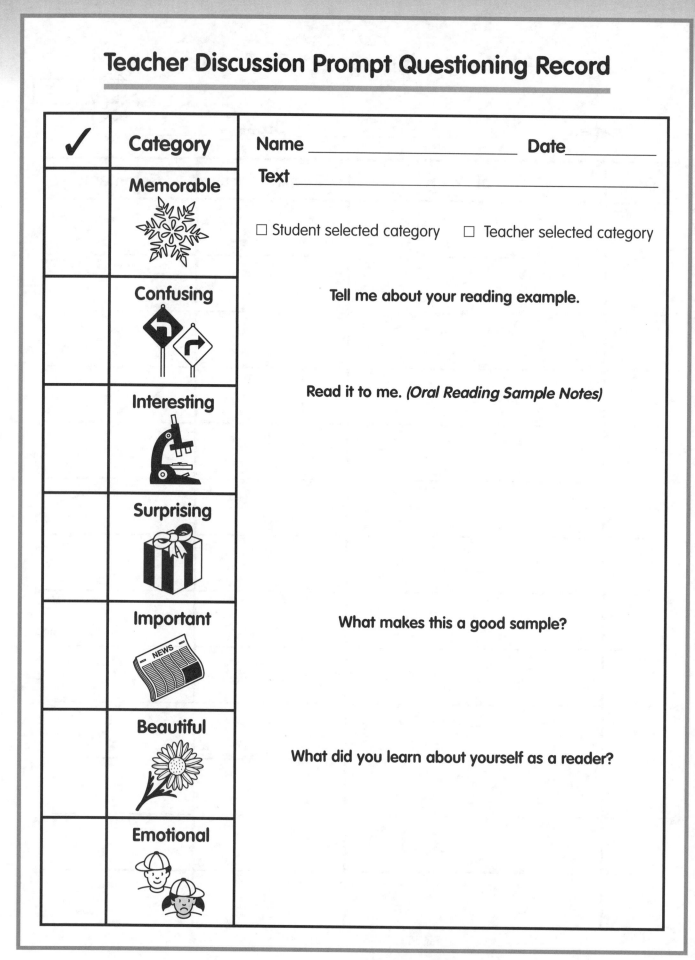

✔	Category
	Memorable
	Confusing
	Interesting
	Surprising
	Important
	Beautiful
	Emotional

Name _____ Date_____

Text _____

☐ Student selected category   ☐ Teacher selected category

Tell me about your reading example.

Read it to me. *(Oral Reading Sample Notes)*

What makes this a good sample?

What did you learn about yourself as a reader?

Comprehension Gestures Planning Form

✓	Gestures	Text Sample to Model Concept	Support Needs
	Big Idea		
	Key Detail		
	Supporting View		
	Opposing View		
	Connection		
	Remember		
	Inference		
	Prediction		
	Confusion		
	Strategy		

Student Strategy Use Reference Form

Strategy	Visual	Specific strategies to reinforce/teaching points
Ask: Does this make sense?		
Look at the picture clues		
Think about what I already know	REWIND STOP FORWARD	
Predict what may be ahead	REWIND STOP FORWARD	
Read between the lines		
Substitute a word and read on	The word is	
Look for chunks I already know	word	
Sound the word out and reread		
Ask someone for help	INFORMATION	
Stop and summarize	STOP	

Student Strategy Use Conferencing Form

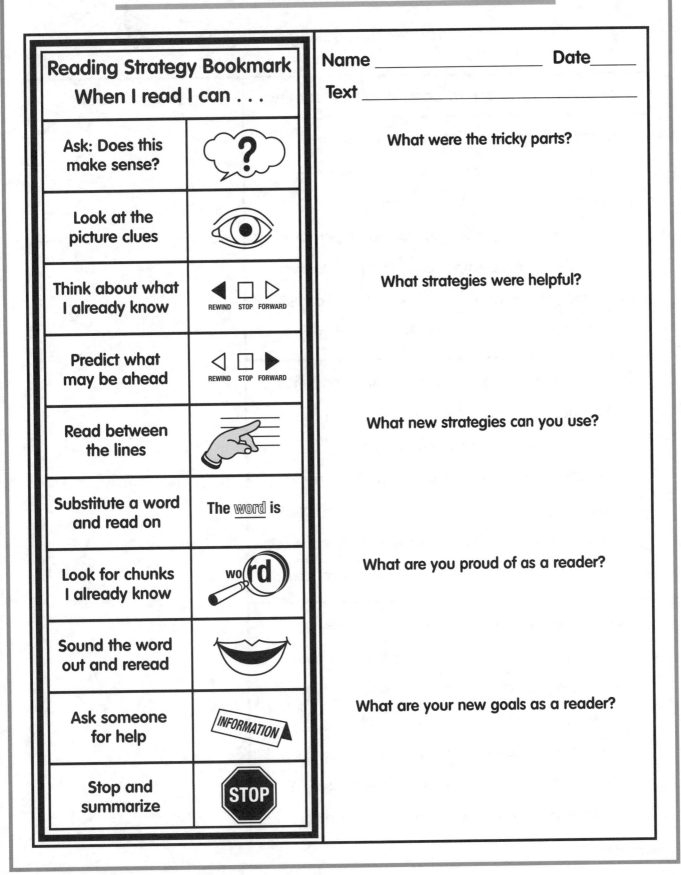

Reading Strategy Bookmark
When I read I can . . .

Ask: Does this make sense?	
Look at the picture clues	
Think about what I already know	REWIND STOP FORWARD
Predict what may be ahead	REWIND STOP FORWARD
Read between the lines	
Substitute a word and read on	The word is
Look for chunks I already know	word
Sound the word out and reread	
Ask someone for help	INFORMATION
Stop and summarize	STOP

Name _____ Date_____

Text _____

What were the tricky parts?

What strategies were helpful?

What new strategies can you use?

What are you proud of as a reader?

What are your new goals as a reader?

Instructional Planning Questions

Interactive Note-taking Strategies

Key questions to ask at each stage of learning	Support Goals
Translating Information into written notes ☐ Can students verbalize what they are learning? ☐ Can students put their ideas in written form? ☐ Can students reduce ideas to key words or phrases? ☐ Can students create simple visuals to support learning? ☐ Do students organize their ideas with bulleted points? ☐ Do concepts reflect sequential ideas as appropriate?	
Sharing notes during peer collaboration activities ☐ Do students review notes before sharing with peers? ☐ Do students refer to written notes during peer sharing? ☐ Do students elaborate on their ideas during sharing? ☐ Do students add what they learn from peers to notes? ☐ Do students restate what they are learning from peers? ☐ Do students use notes as a resource to support ideas?	
Using notes as a long-term resource reference ☐ Do students revisit notes periodically to review ideas? ☐ Can students recall learning points using this resource? ☐ Do students recall important learning without notes? ☐ Do students relate new learning to the note-taking form? ☐ Do students apply learning in other related activities? ☐ Do students use the notes as a study reference?	

Instructional Observations and Support

Three-Section Notes

Topic _____ Date _____

Order (Circle)	Support Level	Key Ideas to Emphasize	Support Needs
1 2 3	Modeled Shared Guided Independent		
1 2 3	Modeled Shared Guided Independent		
1 2 3	Modeled Shared Guided Independent		

Instructional Planning Questions

☐ Brain Facts   ☐ Brain Words

Description of key ideas to emphasize	Support Needs
Important learning facts/words:	
Quick sketches of facts/words:	
Summary overview of key facts/words:	

Instructional Observations and Support

Ear, Eye, Talk Notes

Title/Topic _____ Date _____

Order (Circle)	Overview of Learning Points	Support Needs
👂 1 2 3		
👁 1 2 3		
👄 1 2 3		

Conclusion

Raising the "Power Potential" of Our Instructional Practices

I t's always been hard for me to write conclusions, because I'd much rather think in terms of beginnings. That is, now that you've read through this book I encourage you to begin in whatever way makes sense for you. The forms offer concrete tools to identify, teach, and assess learning concepts across grades or content areas. In another light, they support your ability to manage an effective balance of whole-group, small-group, and independent instruction—all key features of an effective RTI framework. They help you angle your teaching so students take on more responsibility for their learning. But in any light, they are meant to be a menu of options rather than a recipe, so please put your own personal stamp on them. Pay attention to your students as they engage in these activities. In the early stages, model how to put ideas on paper to build a foundation for the future and promote new challenges as students gain increasing independence.

Select specific forms as daily grade-level or schoolwide rituals across the curriculum for a consistent view to support experienced and inexperienced teachers alike. Use professional discussions to target what worked or explore helpful modifications within and across tiers or grades. First-grade teacher Sheri Ramirez in Lakeside, Arizona, suggested using my assessment Stoplight folders to prioritize the forms she wanted to use immediately (green), next (yellow), or later (red). This is an excellent way to personalize the forms to fit your own instructional goals and the specific needs of your students. Imagine discussions that might ensue in or between grade levels as you make these choices together through dialogue that will lead to even more effective teaching.

The major point I want to leave you with is that each of these forms brings out one thing—*student response*. Generally speaking, we need to hear and see more of our students' thinking in the course of the school day, and these activities will give you that opportunity. As we encourage children to lift up their voices, we reinforce their learning, as they show us their wonderfully individual takes on things, and expose what we didn't quite teach well enough. How *we* respond to the work they do on these activities is critical. We can see them as a means to correct their errors and set up only roadblocks to new learning or we can see them as a means to cultivate deeper understandings. We have to possess a new and open mind-set—imagine an open hand filled with possibilities as opposed to a fist closed tightly to the rich options before us.

As I write this, my mind is drawn to Stanford University psychologist Carol Dweck's studies on learning. She found that a crucial ingredient of successful education rests in our ability to help students learn from their mistakes. Lehrer illustrates her findings by stating that focusing on mistakes "leads students to see mistakes as signs of stupidity and not as the building blocks of knowledge" (2009, 52). When we rationalize mistakes as their failure to learn in the name of standards rather than our failure to teach more deeply, we miss the many golden opportunities that abound to help our students learn *how* to learn.

Dweck's findings should be the driving force of these activities. Happy faces, stickers, red marks, and grades only draw attention to mistakes, while dialogue and support guide students to examine these mistakes more closely as a rich springboard to new learning. Effective feedback is rooted in the learning process and is designed to make students *smarter* in any subsequent attempts to repeat or apply learning in other contexts. The open-ended nature of forms makes it easy to highlight these learning opportunities through varied and repeated exposure.

One important way we accomplish this is to use student responses to promote and reinforce the very thinking good readers use naturally. This is not a one-sided proposition, but one that embraces both teaching *and* learning. We model this thinking when we verbalize good strategies at all stages, but this alone is not enough. We must also celebrate the thinking students bring to the literacy task as stated by Harvey and Daniels: "The more kids see that their thinking matters, the more they understand their own power" (2009, 32). Our conversational dialogue promotes both kinds of thinking— our own and our students'—as we learn about students and students learn about learning in each interaction. This is a critical ingredient if our goal is truly moving forward with RTI.

Enjoy the many possibilities this book holds, always maintaining a watchful eye to reinforce successes or support students who flounder. On their own, these activities are only pieces of paper based on the grand ideas of a fellow teacher. The magic comes when we add a heavy dose of the *you* factor by exploring deeper questions to consider what led to student successes, *why* some students aren't successful, and what *you* can do to turn those struggles into successes. The wonderful interaction that inseparably intertwines the teaching and learning process is the ultimate power source that will strengthen suggestions on paper to teaching that is more focused, more engaging, and more effective.

As I said at the beginning of our journey, imagine for a moment that you are holding a lightbulb in your hands. The lightbulb is a remarkable design, but it has little use without a power source. When it is connected to a power source, the lightbulb is instantly illuminated. In the same way, the forms and activity ideas I've created are simply the lightbulb in your hand—but they are useless without a power source. Once again, the you factor comes into play as you power the ideas by carefully choosing just the right text, context, setting, and dialogue most likely to lead to learning. As you share these activities with your students, never lose sight of the fact that you power learning events—and the light shines ever more radiantly the more you engage in the instructional process. Quite an amazing design concept, isn't it?

Shine on little light of mine!

References

Beck, Isabel, and Margaret McKeown. 2006. *Improving Comprehension with Questioning the Author: A Fresh and Expanded View of a Powerful Approach.* New York: Scholastic/Theory, and Practice.

Dorn, Linda, and Barbara Schubert. 2008. "A Comprehensive Intervention Model for Preventing Reading Failure: A Response to Intervention Process." *Journal of Reading Recovery* 7 (2): 29–41.

Fisher, Douglas, and Nancy Frey. 2008. *Better Learning Through Structured Teaching: A Framework for the Gradual Release of Responsibility.* Alexandria, VA: ASCD (Association for Supervision and Curriculum Development).

Frey, Nancy, and Douglas Fisher. 2009. *Learning Words Inside and Out: Vocabulary Instruction That Boosts Achievement in All Subject Areas.* Portsmouth, NH: Heinemann.

Harvey, Stephanie, and Harvey Daniels. 2009. *Comprehension and Collaboration: Inquiry Circles in Action.* Portsmouth, NH: Heinemann.

Howard, Mary. 2009. *RTI from All Sides.* Portsmouth, NH: Heinemann.

Lehrer, Jonah. 2009. *How We Decide.* Boston: Houghton Mifflin Harcourt.

Medina, John. 2009. *Brain Rules: 12 Principles for Surviving and Thriving at Work, Home, and School.* Seattle, WA: Pear Press.

Miller, Debbie. 2002. *Reading with Meaning: Teaching Comprehension in the Primary Grades.* Portland, ME: Stenhouse.

Owocki, Gretchen. 2010. *The RTI Daily Planning Book, K–6.* Portsmouth, NH: Heinemann.

Taberski, Sharon. 2009. *It's All About Comprehension.* Portsmouth, NH: Heinemann.

———. 2011. *Comprehension from the Ground Up: Simplified, Sensible Instruction for the K–3 Reading Workshop.* Portsmouth, NH: Heinemann.

Tomlinson, Carol Ann, and Jay McTighe. 2006. *Integrating Differentiated Instruction and Understanding by Design: Connecting Content and Kids.* Alexandria, VA: ASCD (Association for Supervision and Curriculum Development).